Rust In Practice

Second Edition

*A Programmers Guide to Build Rust Programs,
Test Applications and Create Cargo Packages*

Rick Tim

Copyright © 2024 by GitforGits

Published by: GitforGits

Publisher: Sonal Dhandre

www.gitforgits.com

support@gitforgits.com

Printed in India

First Printing: April 2024

ISBN: 9788119177769

Cover Design by: Kitten Publishing

For permission to use material from this book, please contact GitforGits at support@gitforgits.com.

Prologue

As the proud author of "Rust In Practice, Second Edition," I am overjoyed to take you on a journey through the updated and enlarged review of Rust, a programming language that has had a profound impact on the world right now. This book expands on the topics covered in the first edition, going deeper into practical applications and exploring new features that help Rust mature into a strong tool for system-level programming and beyond.

From the start, my goal was to provide both novice and seasoned developers with a complete overview of Rust's possibilities through a practical lens. We begin by covering Rust's fundamentals—ownership, borrowing, and the type system—which are critical to understanding how Rust achieves memory safety without a garbage collector. Each chapter is designed to build on previous knowledge, ensuring that you understand both the theory and application of Rust's key principles.

We then progress to more difficult topics such as error handling, smart pointers, concurrency, and advanced characteristics. Each topic is supported by real-world examples that show how Rust may be used to build efficient, reliable, and maintainable applications. I've also added a new section on asynchronous programming, which reflects Rust's continued progress in handling concurrent processes more smoothly and effectively.

A key addition to this edition is the in-depth look at Rust's ecosystem, which includes Cargo, Crates, and the huge standard library. Understanding these tools will help you realize Rust's full potential, whether you're creating basic utilities or big software systems.

As we conclude with smart pointers and reference cycles, I highlight Rust's distinct approach to memory management, which is both a problem and an asset in learning the language. In the latter chapters, you will find examples and exercises that will help you understand Rust better and give you the confidence to use it in your own projects or as part of your contributions to open-source software.

"Rust In Practice, Second Edition" is more than simply a guidebook; it's an exploration of a language that stresses safety, speed, and concurrency. It is intended for developers who are interested in furthering their Rust knowledge, as well as those who are just getting started but want to go deep. As we conclude, I hope it serves not just as an educational resource, but also as an illustration to which you will return as you progress in your Rust adventure. The future of system programming is bright, so long as we continue to produce stable software that challenges conventional wisdom.

Content

Preface

"Rust In Practice, Second Edition" is an updated book that builds on the previous edition's excellent foundation and is intended to help readers progress from novice to proficient Rust developers. This new version goes deeper into Rust's core and advanced capabilities, making it suitable for learners at all levels.

Beginning with a basic introduction to Rust syntax and semantics, the Second Edition provides a clearer and more detailed explanation of Rust's distinctive ownership model and type system. Readers will thoroughly explore control flow, error management, and Rust's main data types, laying a solid foundation for more advanced topics.

The book includes additional chapters on smart pointers, sophisticated error handling techniques, and the complexities of concurrency and parallelism, which address real-world programming issues. The book covers how to incorporate asynchronous programming features into projects, how to utilize and maintain Cargo, and a more in-depth look at Rust's standard library and the external crates ecosystem.

"Rust In Practice, Second Edition" is intended to serve as both a learning tool and a reference for developing high-performance applications. It is packed with professional advice, clear explanations, and practical examples. This book will not only teach you Rust programming, but it will also help you design software that is strong, simple, efficient, and easily maintainable.

In this book you will learn how to:

- Master Cargo and its extensive command suite to streamline project builds and dependency management.

- Deepen your grasp of Rust's type system, emphasizing ownership and borrowing to efficiently manage memory.

- Utilize advanced traits and generics to create flexible, reusable software components.

- Leverage closures, iterators, and asynchronous programming for high-performance, multi-threaded applications.

- Utilize collections, enhance string operations, and execute effective I/O.

- Explore sophisticated macro usage for metaprogramming and strategies to avoid unsafe code.

- 75+ practical examples showcasing Rust's latest features and best practices.

- Apply rigorous testing methods across diverse Rust applications, with new testing frameworks and methodologies.

GitforGits

Prerequisites

Whether you are just starting your Rust journey or looking to deepen your existing Rust programming skills, this book serves as a practical, example-guided book on your everyday working desk.

Codes Usage

Are you in need of some helpful code examples to assist you in your programming and documentation? Look no further! Our book offers a wealth of supplemental material, including code examples and exercises.

Not only is this book here to aid you in getting your job done, but you have our permission to use the example code in your programs and documentation. However, please note that if you are reproducing a significant portion of the code, we do require you to contact us for permission.

But don't worry, using several chunks of code from this book in your program or answering a question by citing our book and quoting example code does not require permission. But if you do choose to give credit, an attribution typically includes the title, author, publisher, and ISBN. For example, "Rust In Practice, Second Edition by Rick Tim".

If you are unsure whether your intended use of the code examples falls under fair use or the permissions outlined above, please do not hesitate to reach out to us at support@gitforgits.com.

We are happy to assist and clarify any concerns.

Acknowledgement

I owe a tremendous debt of gratitude to GitforGits, for their unflagging enthusiasm and wise counsel throughout the entire process of writing this book. Their knowledge and careful editing helped make sure the piece was useful for people of all reading levels and comprehension skills. In addition, I'd like to thank everyone involved in the publishing process for their efforts in making this book a reality. Their efforts, from copyediting to advertising, made the project what it is today.

Finally, I'd like to express my gratitude to everyone who has shown me unconditional love and encouragement throughout my life. Their support was crucial to the completion of this book. I appreciate your help with this endeavour and your continued interest in my career.

CHAPTER 1: WHY RUST?

Why Rust?

Rust, a powerful tool that has a lot of potential that hasn't been fully realised yet, is available to those who are interested in programming and puts a lot of power in their hands. Rust is a modern programming language that has been gaining a reputation for its focus on safety and performance. It was first introduced in 2010 by Graydon Hoare at Mozilla Research, with contributions from Dave Herman, Brendan Eich, and others. Rust is a low-level language, which means that programmes written in it are close to the hardware of the system and have the ability to produce code that is highly efficient. This is because Rust was designed to be a general-purpose, general-purpose programming language. Rust offers exceptional performance, with code that, on average, runs noticeably faster when compared to code written in other languages.

Rust's primary appeal lies in its promise of memory safety without sacrificing performance. Memory safety means that the language prevents bugs that lead to crashes or security vulnerabilities due to mishandled memory, such as buffer overflows, null pointer dereferencing, and data races in concurrent operations. These guarantees are enforced at compile-time, without the overhead of a runtime or garbage collector, through Rust's ownership system, borrowing, and lifetimes concepts. This means developers spend less time debugging elusive memory-related bugs and more time focusing on the logic and performance of their applications.

Concurrency in software allows multiple sequences of operations to be run in overlapping periods. Rust's approach to concurrency is fearless, meaning it's designed to be done without fear of the common pitfalls associated with it in other languages. Rust achieves this through its ownership and type systems, which statically prevent data races. This allows developers to write more robust applications with parallel processing capabilities, which is an essential feature in the modern age of multi-core and distributed computing.

Rust provides performance akin to that of C and C++, which has historically made these languages the go-to for systems-level programming where control over hardware and memory is necessary. Rust accomplishes this while ensuring safety and modern conveniences. For performance-critical software — from operating systems to game engines to scientific computing applications — Rust delivers the speed and efficiency needed without the usual risks associated with low-level languages.

Rust comes with excellent developer tooling. Cargo, Rust's package manager and build system, simplifies many tasks associated with managing dependencies, compiling packages, and distributing software. This ecosystem makes it easy for developers to share libraries, streamline their build processes, and manage multiple projects with ease. Moreover, Rust's compiler is renowned for its helpful error messages that not only tell you what went wrong but also suggest how to fix it.

The Rust community is known for being exceptionally welcoming and vibrant. It is a community that values learning and development, as evidenced by the plethora of resources available for beginners and experts alike. As Rust has grown in popularity, so has its ecosystem of third-party libraries, tools, and frameworks, which has expanded the language's applications to web development, embedded systems, and more.

As more companies start to adopt Rust due to its benefits in safety and performance, the demand for developers skilled in Rust is growing. Knowledge of Rust can open doors to opportunities in industries that value high-performance applications and secure software solutions. Being proficient in Rust can set a developer apart in the job market, especially in areas like systems programming, web development, and more.

Before we begin in detail about Rust, let me tell you one big thing is that learning Rust is a strategic move for any developer looking to enhance their skills in modern software development. It offers a blend of performance, safety, and modern tooling that is hard to find in other programming languages. Rust not only prepares developers to tackle current software challenges but also equips them to handle future developments in a world where concurrency and safety are becoming increasingly important.

Rust Over Other Programming Languages?

Rust is superior to many other programming languages in a number of respects. It is often compared with other popular programming languages such as Python, C++, and Go, each of which has its unique strengths and is suited for different programming needs and scenarios.

Why Choose Rust Over Python?

Performance

Python is an interpreted language known for its ease of use and speed of development but often at the cost of runtime performance. It is dynamically typed and uses a global interpreter lock (GIL), which can become a bottleneck in CPU-bound and multi-threaded code. In contrast, Rust is a compiled language that offers performance comparable to C and C++. Its powerful concurrency features allow it to excel in performance-critical applications where Python might struggle, such as in system programming, embedded systems, and large-scale data processing where tight control over resources is necessary.

Concurrency

Python's concurrency is hindered by the GIL, which allows only one thread to execute Python bytecodes at a time. This makes true parallelism difficult, though it can be mitigated by using processes instead of threads. Rust, on the other hand, was designed from the ground up with concurrency in mind. Its ownership and type system ensure that data races are compile-time errors, making it easier and safer to write multi-threaded applications.

Memory Management

Python automates memory management through a garbage collector, which simplifies development but can lead to unpredictability in performance, particularly in latency-sensitive applications. Rust provides deterministic management of resources with its system of ownership and borrowing, coupled with zero-cost abstractions, which means you can write low-level code without the overhead typically associated with such control.

Safety

Rust's biggest selling point is its promise of memory safety without using a garbage collector. Python, while safe from the typical memory corruption vulnerabilities found in C and C++, is still prone to runtime errors that Rust compiles out, such as accessing or modifying data in a way that is inconsistent with its ownership rules.

Why Rust Over C++?

Memory Safety

C++ allows great control over system resources and memory, but this flexibility comes at the cost of safety. Memory bugs, buffer overflows, and other vulnerabilities are common in C++ applications, requiring developers to manage memory very carefully. Rust provides similar levels of control as C++ but enforces memory safety at compile time through its ownership rules, eliminating a whole class of bugs that C++ developers constantly have to guard against.

Modern Tooling

Rust comes with Cargo, its package manager and build system, which greatly simplifies dependency management, project compilation, and building tasks that can be cumbersome in C++. Rust's compiler, **rustc**, provides extremely useful error messages which not only tell what is wrong but often suggest multiple ways to fix the problem, improving the developer experience significantly.

Concurrency

C++11 and later have improved support for concurrency, but using these features correctly is often complex and error-prone. Rust's approach to concurrency is not an afterthought but a fundamental aspect of the language, making it much easier to develop robust and scalable multi-threaded applications without fear of data races.

Community and Modern Practices

Rust encourages modern programming practices such as functional programming alongside imperative programming, which can lead to more robust, readable, and maintainable code. The Rust community is very active and places a strong emphasis on inclusivity and safety, both in terms of software and community interaction, which can be very appealing for new developers.

Why Rust Over Go?

Zero-Cost Abstractions

Go is known for its simplicity and efficiency, as well as its excellent support for concurrency through goroutines. However, Rust offers zero-cost abstractions, which means that abstractions you build in Rust compile to assembly with no additional runtime cost, similar to how you would write it in C or C++. This allows developers to write high-level abstractions while keeping the performance of low-level code.

Memory Safety and Fine-Grained Control

Go uses a garbage collector which simplifies development but can introduce latency issues at runtime. Rust's ownership model eliminates the need for a garbage collector and provides more predictable performance along with fine-grained control over memory management, similar to C and C++.

Type System and Generics

Rust's type system is more sophisticated than Go's, especially when it comes to generics and trait-based generics. Rust allows for more expressive and flexible code without sacrificing performance. Go's type system is simpler, which can be an advantage for smaller projects and teams but might be limiting for more complex systems.

Advanced Features

Rust supports advanced features such as pattern matching, advanced error handling, and macros, which can significantly reduce boilerplate and improve the expressiveness and robustness of code. While Go favors simplicity, which has its advantages, Rust's rich feature set is geared towards tackling complex programming tasks more effectively.

To quickly summarize, if you wish to prioritize safety, performance, and modern tooling, and if your project involves complex systems where control over memory and concurrency is critical, Rust offers compelling advantages. Its learning curve is steeper compared to Python and Go, and perhaps similar to C++, but the benefits of mastering Rust, especially for systems programming and performance-critical applications, are considerable.

Rust Syntax

Rust's design emphasizes safety, performance, and concise syntax, which makes it an appealing choice for developers coming from various programming backgrounds. Below, we'll explore some foundational elements of Rust programming: variables, functions, control flow, structs, and traits.

Variables

Variables are immutable by default, promoting safer code practices. However, Rust also supports mutable variables when necessary. The compiler's ability to infer types can simplify code, though explicit typing can enhance readability and maintain consistency in larger codebases.

```
let x = 5; // Immutable integer, type i32 inferred

let mut y = 3.14; // Mutable floating-point number, type
f64 inferred

let name = "John"; // Immutable string slice, type &str
inferred
```

The above code snippet demonstrates the use of type inference, while the **mut** keyword indicates that **y** can be changed after its initial assignment.

Functions

Functions in Rust are defined with the **fn** keyword, followed by a name, parameters, and a return type. Rust encourages explicit declaration of the return type which aids in maintaining clear and predictable function signatures.

```
fn add(x: i32, y: i32) -> i32 {

 x + y // Implicit return (no semicolon), returns the sum
of x and y

}
```

This function demonstrates an implicit return, a feature that allows the last expression in a block to automatically be used as the return value, provided it isn't followed by a semicolon.

Control Flow

Rust's control flow constructs are robust and familiar to those experienced with other C-like languages. It includes conditional **if-else** statements, loops, and **match** statements, which are akin to switch-case statements but more powerful.

```
let x = 5;
```

```rust
if x > 0 {

 println!("x is positive");

} else {

 println!("x is negative or zero");

}


// Demonstrating a controlled loop with a break condition

loop {

 println!("This loop will intentionally run only once for
demonstration.");

 break;

}


let y = 5;


match y {

 1 => println!("y is 1"),

 2 => println!("y is 2"),

 _ => println!("y is something else"), // catch-all
pattern

}
```

In the above, **if-else** and **match** are used to handle conditional logic, while the **loop** is used to demonstrate an infinite loop that can be controlled by internal logic (**break**).

Structs

Structs allow you to create custom data types with related fields. They form the building blocks for more complex data structures in your programs.

```rust
struct Point {

  x: i32,

  y: i32,

}


let p = Point { x: 5, y: 10 };

println!("Point coordinates: ({}, {})", p.x, p.y);
```

This struct **Point** demonstrates how custom types are declared and instantiated in Rust.

Traits

Traits are used to define functionality that multiple types can implement, similar to interfaces in other languages but with the added benefit of greater flexibility and power.

```rust
trait Animal {

  fn make_sound(&self) -> &'static str;

}



struct Dog;



impl Animal for Dog {
```

```
fn make_sound(&self) -> &'static str {

"bark"

}

}



let dog = Dog;

println!("The dog says {}", dog.make_sound());
```

The above code snippet shows how to define a trait **Animal** and implement it for the **Dog** struct, allowing for polymorphic behavior on types that share the same trait.

Writing 'Hello world'

Writing a "Hello, World!" program is a traditional way to start learning a new language, as it provides a simple yet complete example of a language's syntax for functions and output operations.

Rust is a statically typed language, meaning you often define the type of variables explicitly, though Rust's compiler is also capable of inferring types to make the code cleaner.

For example:

```
let x: i32 = 5;

let y: f64 = 3.14;
```

In the above, **x** and **y** are declared with specific types, but Rust's type inference allows you to omit these when it's clear. We shall revisit the function **add** for adding two integers:

```
fn add(a: i32, b: i32) -> i32 {

a + b

}
```

This function demonstrates basic function syntax in Rust, including parameter type declarations and the return type.

Rust's ownership principles are foundational, enforcing memory safety without a garbage collector. This system ensures that each value in Rust has a singular owner, and the memory is automatically reclaimed once the owner goes out of scope, preventing common bugs such as dangling pointers.

The Rust macro system extends the language's capabilities, allowing custom constructs that can behave like built-in features. Macros are powerful tools for metaprogramming in Rust.

Let us now implement the quintessential "Hello, World!" program. This program will leverage Rust's **println!** macro to print a message to the console. Given below is a basic implementation:

```
fn main() {

 println!("Hello, world!");

}
```

To run this program, you use Rust's package manager and build system, Cargo. Cargo handles many tasks, including building your code, downloading the libraries it depends on, and building those libraries.

Given below are the steps to execute the "Hello, World!" program:

- Open your terminal and run **cargo new hello_world**. This command creates a new directory called **hello_world** with a Cargo.toml file (which describes your project and its dependencies) and a **src** directory with a main.rs file.

- Open the **src/main.rs** file and replace its contents with the "Hello, World!" program shown above.

- Back in your terminal, navigate to your project directory (**cd hello_world**) and run **cargo run**. Cargo will compile your program and then run it, printing "Hello, world!" to the console.

This simple hello world program quickly makes us practice several of Rust's key features: its package management, its emphasis on safety through controlled memory management, and its use of macros.

My First Program: A Simple Calculator

Now that we have covered the fundamentals of Rust programming, it is time to put those skills to use by developing a basic application. In this section, you will learn how to construct a calculator application using only a few lines of code.

To create a simple calculator program in Rust, you can follow these steps:

Setting up the Project

Start by creating a new Rust project using Cargo, which will help manage and build your project:

```
cargo new calculator
```

This command sets up a new folder named **calculator** with a standard Rust project structure including a **Cargo.toml** for managing dependencies and a **src** directory for your source files.

Writing Main Program

Open the **main.rs** file inside the **src** directory and set up your project to receive and process user input. Following is the main function with detailed comments:

```
use std::io; // Importing the I/O library for input
handling


fn main() {

 println!("Welcome to the calculator!");


 loop {

 println!("Enter an expression to calculate (e.g., 2 +
2), or type 'exit' to quit:");


  let mut input = String::new(); // String to store user
input
```

```
io::stdin().read_line(&mut input).expect("Failed to read
input");

let input = input.trim(); // Trim whitespace


if input.eq("exit") {

println!("Goodbye!");

break; // Exit loop and program

}


let result = calculate(input).unwrap_or_else(|err| {

println!("Error: {}", err);

0.0

});

println!("Result: {}", result);

}

}
```

Implementing Calculation Logic

To perform calculations, you'll parse the user's input and evaluate the expression. Below is the **calculate** function enhanced with complete error handling and the ability to process basic arithmetic operations:

```
use regex::Regex;
```

```rust
fn calculate(input: &str) -> Result<f64, &'static str> {

 let re = Regex::new(r"([\d.]+)\s*([+-
/*])\s*([\d.]+)").expect("Invalid regex");

 let captures = re.captures(input).ok_or("Invalid input
format")?;


 let num1: f64 = captures[1].parse().map_err(|_| "Invalid
number")?;

 let num2: f64 = captures[3].parse().map_err(|_| "Invalid
number")?;

 let op = captures[2].chars().next().ok_or("Invalid
operator")?;


 match op {

 '+' => Ok(num1 + num2),

 '-' => Ok(num1 - num2),

 '*' => Ok(num1 * num2),

 '/' => num2.abs() > 0.0.then(|| num1 /
num2).ok_or("Cannot divide by zero"),

 _ => Err("Unsupported operator"),

 }

}
```

This implementation uses the **Regex** library to split the user input into operands and an operator. It handles errors gracefully, returning a **Result** type that either contains the calculation result or an error message. Do verify to include the **regex** crate in your **Cargo.toml**:

```
[dependencies]

regex = "1"
```

Testing the Calculator

With the program now complete, you can build and run your project using Cargo:

```
cargo run
```

This command compiles the project and runs it, allowing you to interactively test the calculator functionality from the command line.

This simple calculator serves as a practical application of your Rust programming skills, integrating various concepts like string manipulation, regular expressions, error handling, and user input. Through this project, you've seen how to build a responsive command-line application.

Summary

This chapter focused on the compelling reasons to choose Rust as a programming language, emphasizing its unique approach to safety, performance, and concurrency. Here's a consolidated summary of the learnings from this chapter:

Rust is recognized for offering both safety and high performance without the need for a garbage collector, which is unique among system programming languages. This safety is guaranteed through its ownership system, borrowing, and lifetimes concept, ensuring that memory safety errors like buffer overflows and null pointer dereferences are caught at compile time. Concurrency is another strong suit of Rust, designed to be fearless with built-in support to prevent data races, which are common in other languages when handling concurrent operations. This makes Rust suitable for applications requiring high performance across modern multi-core processors.

The ecosystem surrounding Rust, including its package manager Cargo, simplifies project management by handling compilation and managing dependencies efficiently. Rust's compiler is notably helpful, providing clear and actionable error messages that aid in debugging.

The chapter also compares Rust with other popular programming languages like Python, C++, and Go, highlighting Rust's advantages in performance, memory safety, and concurrency. This makes Rust a strategic choice for developers aiming to enhance their skills and tackle complex, performance-critical applications effectively.

Overall, the chapter establishes Rust as a powerful tool for modern software development, equipped to handle both current and future programming challenges due to its design and community support.

CHAPTER 2: GETTING READY WITH RUST ENVIRONMENT

Introduction

Whatever operating system you are using, this chapter will walk you through the necessary setup to start programming in Rust with ease. This chapter starts with a detailed walkthrough of installing Rust using rustup, a toolchain manager that streamlines the installation of rustc, cargo, and other required components. You can easily get Rust running on your Windows or Linux machine by following the installation instructions that are specific to your platform.

Utilizing Cargo, which is critical for managing Rust projects, becomes the primary focus once Rust is installed. Cargo manages project builds and dependencies using Rust packages called crates. To help you build applications, like a basic calculator program, you'll find out how to add and manage these crates. Crates can add functionality, like command-line parsing or advanced mathematical operations, to your program.

Additionally, the chapter delves into the process of configuring the widely used code editor Visual Studio Code (VS Code), which offers extensions that are compatible with Rust. This section of the chapter walks you through the process of installing VS Code and setting it up with extensions that are specific to Rust. These extensions will improve your coding experience and add powerful features like code completion and debugging.

You will have all the necessary tools to start building your own Rust applications, as well as a fully functional Rust development environment tailored to your OS, by the end of this chapter. This groundwork will prepare you for success in your Rust programming endeavors by covering not only installation but also how to effectively utilize Rust's ecosystem. To guarantee that developers have the knowledge and resources to build efficient and resilient applications, this chapter is essential for laying a firm groundwork for Rust development.

Setting up Rust on Windows

A few simple steps get you ready to write and run Rust code efficiently by setting up a Rust development environment on Windows. For Windows users, this is a must-have in order to use Rust's secure concurrency features and powerful system programming capabilities. On Windows, you can follow the below steps:

Downloading and Installing Rust

Begin by navigating to the official Rust website and click on the "Get Started" button. This leads you to the setup instructions, where you can download the **rustup-init.exe** installer for Windows. Running this installer will install the latest version of Rust, which includes **rustc** (the Rust compiler), **cargo** (the Rust package manager), and the standard library.

Verifying the Installation

After installation, it's good practice to ensure that Rust has been installed correctly. Open the Command Prompt and type:

```
rustc --version
```

This command checks and displays the installed version of Rust, confirming that Rust is ready to use on your system.

Setting up Development Environment

For writing Rust code, you'll need an Integrated Development Environment (IDE) or a powerful text editor. VS Code is highly recommended due to its robust support for Rust via extensions like the Rust Language Server (RLS) or rust-analyzer, which provide features like syntax highlighting, code completion, and debugging tools.

To install VS Code, visit the website and download the Windows installer. Follow the prompts to install it on your system.

Creating first Rust Project

With your editor set up, you can now create a new Rust project using Cargo. Open your Command Prompt and run:

```
cargo new myproject
```

This command creates a new directory called **myproject** with a basic Rust project structure:

- **Cargo.toml** — a configuration file for managing your project's metadata and dependencies.
- **src/main.rs** — a default source file where you can start writing your Rust code.

Navigate into your project directory with **cd myproject**, and you can open the entire directory in VS Code by typing:

```
code .
```

Building and Running Project

To compile and run your project, use the following Cargo command:

```
cargo run
```

This command compiles the code in your project and runs the resulting executable. For a new project, the default code in **src/main.rs** will print "Hello, world!" to the terminal.

Now that your Rust environment is configured, consider exploring further:

- Write basic Rust programs, such as a "hello, world" or a simple calculator, to get a feel for the syntax and tools.

- Dive into Rust's unique features like the ownership and borrowing system, which are fundamental to Rust's approach to memory management.

- Explore Rust's macro system for metaprogramming to see how you can extend the language's capabilities.

Setting up Rust on Linux

Updating System

Before installing any new software, it's a good practice to update your package listings and upgrade the existing packages to their latest versions. You can do this with the following commands:

```
sudo apt update

sudo apt upgrade
```

This ensures that all dependencies installed are compatible with the latest available versions.

Installing Build Essentials

Rust requires a linker and other build tools, which are available in the **build-essential** package on Debian-based distributions like Ubuntu. Install it by running:

```
sudo apt install build-essential
```

This package includes the GCC compiler, **make** and other essential tools required for compiling C and C++ programs, which are sometimes needed for compiling Rust dependencies.

Installing Rust using Rustup

Rustup is the recommended tool for installing Rust. It allows you to manage multiple versions of Rust and its associated tools easily. To install Rustup and the latest stable version of Rust, run the following command:

```
curl --proto '=https' --tlsv1.2 -sSf https://sh.rustup.rs
| sh
```

Then, follow the on-screen instructions to complete the installation. Typically, you should select option 1 to install the stable version, which is suitable for most users.

Verifying Rust Installation

Once Rustup has completed the installation, you can verify it by checking the version of Rust installed:

```
rustc --version
```

This command should output the version number of Rust, confirming that the installation was successful.

Setting up Environment Path

To use Rust from any location in your terminal, add Rust's bin directory to your PATH environment variable:

```
echo 'export PATH="$HOME/.cargo/bin:$PATH"' >> ~/.bashrc

source ~/.bashrc
```

This command adds the path to the Rust installation to your shell profile script and applies the changes.

With Rust installed on your Linux system, you are ready to start exploring Rust programming. You might want to start by creating a simple project using Cargo, Rust's package manager and build tool, which you installed along with Rust:

```
cargo new hello_world

cd hello_world

cargo run
```

This set of commands creates a new Rust project named **hello_world**, builds it, and runs the resulting executable, which will print "Hello, world!" to the console.

Installing Crates and Cargo on Windows

In order to manage Rust projects and install crates on Windows, it is necessary to have the Rust compiler and Cargo, the Rust package manager, correctly installed.

Installing Rust Compiler

First, confirm that you have the Rust compiler installed. Open Command Prompt and run:

```
rustc --version
```

This command checks if Rust is installed and displays the installed version. If Rust is not installed, download it from the official Rust website:

- Visit https://www.rust-lang.org/
- Click on the "Get Started" button.
- Follow the link to download the Rust installer for Windows.
- Execute the downloaded **.exe** file and follow the on-screen instructions. During the installation:
  - Accept the license agreement.
  - Choose the destination folder.
  - Ensure you choose to install Rust with the default settings, which include Cargo.

Setting up Rust Environment

After installing Rust, set the default Rust toolchain to the stable version to ensure compatibility and stability across your projects:

```
rustup default stable
```

This command configures Rustup, which manages Rust versions, to use the stable toolchain by default.

Verifying Cargo Installation

Cargo is bundled with the Rust installation. To verify Cargo is installed:

```
cargo --version
```

This will output the version of Cargo installed, confirming it's ready for use.

Using Cargo to Install Crates

With Cargo installed, you can easily manage dependencies and install libraries (crates). To install a crate, navigate to your project's root directory in Command Prompt and use:

```
cargo install crate_name
```

Replace **crate_name** with the name of the crate you wish to install. For example, to install the popular **serde** crate for serialization and deserialization, you would use:

```
cargo install serde
```

Cargo will handle downloading, building, and configuring the crate to be used within your project.

Include Crates in Project

After installing a crate, to use it in your Rust files, include it at the top of your file with:

```
extern crate crate_name;
```

Replace **crate_name** with the actual name of the installed crate.

Following this setup, you will have a fully functional Rust development environment on Windows, including the compiler and Cargo.

Installing Crates and Cargo on Linux

After installing Rust through rustup, it's essential to configure the Rust environment to use the appropriate version of the Rust toolchain. Open your terminal and execute:

```
rustup default stable
```

This command sets the stable version as the default Rust toolchain. If needed, you can switch to other versions like beta or nightly by replacing **stable** with **beta** or **nightly**.

Installing Crate with Cargo

To install a new crate using Cargo, use the **cargo install** command followed by the name of the crate. For example, to install the **clap** crate, which is widely used for parsing command-line arguments, run:

```
cargo install clap
```

This command downloads and installs the **clap** crate along with its dependencies. If you need a specific version of the crate, you can specify it using the **--version** flag:

```
cargo install clap --version 2.33.0
```

Using Crate in Project

To utilize an installed crate in your Rust project, you must declare it in your **Cargo.toml** file under the **[dependencies]** section. For instance, to add **clap**:

```
[dependencies]

clap = "2.33.0"
```

This inclusion informs Cargo to manage **clap** as a project dependency, ensuring it's available when you build your project. In your Rust source files, you can then use the crate by importing it at the beginning of your files:

```
use clap::{App, Arg};
```

This statement makes the specified modules available in your code, allowing you to leverage **clap** for handling command-line inputs effectively.

Following these steps, you should now have crates and Cargo installed and configured on your Linux machine. Cargo streamlines the process of managing dependencies in Rust projects, which facilitates the upkeep and modification of libraries utilized by your applications.

Installing Visual Studio (VS) Code on Window

Downloading and Installing VS Code

- To start, download VS Code from the official website.
- Click the "Download" button and select the Windows installer.

- Once downloaded, run the installer and follow the on-screen instructions to complete the installation. This typically involves agreeing to the license, choosing an installation directory, and possibly selecting additional tasks such as adding a shortcut to the PATH or creating a desktop icon.

Installing Rust Extension in VS Code

With VS Code installed, the next step is to add support for Rust:

- Open VS Code.

- Navigate to the "Extensions" view by clicking on the square icon on the sidebar or pressing **Ctrl+Shift+X**.

- In the search bar, type "Rust" and press Enter.

- Find the "Rust" extension by rust-lang (official extension) or another popular Rust extension like "Rust Analyzer" which is highly recommended for its powerful features and ease of use.

- Click "Install" on your chosen Rust extension. This extension will provide features such as syntax highlighting, code completion, and linting, enhancing your coding experience.

Configuring Rust Extension

After installing the Rust extension, configure it to use the specific paths for Rust's tools:

- Open the Command Prompt and run:

```
rustup show
```

- This command displays the active Rust toolchain's details, including the installation paths for **rustc** (the compiler) and **cargo** (the package manager).

- Copy the displayed paths.

- In VS Code, go to "File" > "Preferences" > "Settings" (or press **Ctrl+,**).

- Search for "Rust" settings within VS Code. Depending on the extension, you might need to configure paths for **rustc** and **cargo** if the extension doesn't automatically detect them.

- Paste the paths into the appropriate fields if necessary.

Testing Setup

To ensure everything is set up correctly:

- In VS Code, create a new folder and open it.
- Open the integrated terminal (`Ctrl+``) and run:

```
cargo init
```

- This initializes a new Rust project with a basic directory structure and a **Cargo.toml** file.
- VS Code and the installed Rust extension should recognize the Rust project and activate relevant features like autocompletion and inline error messages.

Using VS Code, you have successfully set up a fully functional Rust development environment on your Windows PC. Get your feet wet with Rust projects in VS Code and take advantage of its robust editing, debugging, and code management capabilities.

Installing VS Code on Linux

Downloading VS Code

First, visit the official website and navigate to the download section.

Choose the "Linux" option from the dropdown menu to download the appropriate VS Code package for your distribution. The download will typically be a **.tar.gz** file, suitable for various Linux distributions.

Installing VS Code

To install the downloaded package, you'll need to extract it and run the installer:

- Open a terminal window.
- Navigate to the directory where the VS Code package was downloaded.
- Extract the package with the command:

```
tar -xvf code_*.tar.gz
```

- This command decompresses the files into a new directory. Navigate to this directory.
- Inside this directory, run:

```
./code
```

- This command will start VS Code.

Installing Rust Extension

After VS Code is up and running:

- Click on the "Extensions" icon in the left sidebar or press **Ctrl+Shift+X**.

- Type "Rust" in the search bar and press Enter.

- Select an appropriate Rust extension, such as "Rust" by rust-lang or "Rust Analyzer," and click on the "Install" button.

Configuring Rust Extension

To ensure the Rust extension operates with your system's Rust installation:

- Open a terminal and check your Rust setup:

```
rustup show
```

- This command displays the active Rust toolchain paths.

- Copy the path to the Rust compiler (**rustc**) and Cargo, displayed by the command.

- In VS Code, go to "File" > "Preferences" > "Settings" (or press **Ctrl+,**).

- Search for "Rust" settings and find the configuration options for the Rust toolchain.

- Paste the paths into the "Path to Rustc" and "Path to Cargo" fields as appropriate.

Testing Installation

To confirm everything is set up correctly:

- In VS Code, go to "File" > "New Folder", create a new folder, and open it.

- Right-click the folder in VS Code and select "Open with Code".

- Open the integrated terminal in VS Code (`Ctrl+``) and initiate a new Rust project:

```
cargo init
```

- This command creates a basic Rust project with a **Cargo.toml** and a **src/main.rs** file.
- The Rust extension should automatically recognize the Rust project and activate features like code completion and linting.

Using Crate 'clap' for Calculator Program

To show how crates can simplify and improve the functionality of a program, we now learn to rewrite the calculator program. To make our calculator more powerful and easy to use, we will utilize the **clap** crate for parsing arguments passed in via the command line.

Setting up the Project

First, create a new project if you haven't already:

```
cargo new calculator

cd calculator
```

Adding Dependencies

Open the **Cargo.toml** file and add **clap** to the dependencies section. This crate simplifies parsing command-line arguments:

```
[dependencies]

clap = "2.33.3"
```

Writing Calculator Program

We modify the **main.rs** file to use **clap** for handling input. We'll also improve the calculate function to handle basic arithmetic operations:

```
use clap::{App, Arg};



fn main() {
```

```rust
let matches = App::new("Calculator")

.version("1.0")

.author("Your Name")

.about("Performs basic arithmetic")

.arg(Arg::with_name("operation")

.help("The operation to perform; format should be
'<num1> <operator> <num2>'")

.required(true)

.index(1))

.get_matches();


let operation = matches.value_of("operation").unwrap();

match calculate(operation) {

Ok(result) => println!("Result: {}", result),

Err(e) => eprintln!("Error: {}", e),

}

}


fn calculate(input: &str) -> Result<f64, &'static str> {

let tokens: Vec<&str> =
input.split_whitespace().collect();

if tokens.len() != 3 {
```

```
        return Err("Input must be a binary operation like '2 +
2'");

    }



    let num1 = tokens[0].parse::<f64>().map_err(|_| "Invalid
number")?;

    let operator = tokens[1];

    let num2 = tokens[2].parse::<f64>().map_err(|_| "Invalid
number")?;


    match operator {

    "+" => Ok(num1 + num2),

    "-" => Ok(num1 - num2),

    "*" => Ok(num1 * num2),

    "/" => if num2 != 0.0 { Ok(num1 / num2) } else {
Err("Cannot divide by zero") },

    _ => Err("Unsupported operator"),

    }

}
```

In the above program,

- The **clap** crate is used to define a simple CLI that expects one argument, the operation to perform. It parses the command line input when you run your program and extracts the operation string.

- The **calculate** function now splits the input string into components (number1, operator, number2), validates and parses them, and performs the specified arithmetic operation. It also handles errors like invalid input or division by zero more gracefully.

- The program uses **Result** to handle potential errors that can occur during parsing numbers or performing operations. This way, the program can provide meaningful error messages and avoid panicking.

Running the Program

Compile and run the program with:

```
cargo run -- "10 / 2"
```

This command passes the operation **"10 / 2"** to your calculator, and it should output **Result: 5**.

When you use crates like **clap**, you can build strong applications that scale well with complexity and command-line arguments are a breeze to handle. Your programs will be more user-and maintainer-friendly with this method's improved error management and drastic reduction of boilerplate code.

Summary

This chapter focused on creating a stable Rust development environment that works on several operating systems, so developers may easily start developing and running Rust code. Starting with rustup, a toolchain manager that makes managing Rust versions and related tools easier, the chapter walked users through installing Rust. Here you may find comprehensive instructions for installing Rust on Linux and Windows. For Linux users, we highlight the significance of installing build-essential and updating system packages.

If you are using Windows, this chapter will walk you through every step of getting the Rust compiler and package manager, Cargo, from the official Rust website. It also went over setting up the Rust environment, which involves adding Rust to the system's PATH. This makes it possible to run Rust commands from any directory in the command line.

The following tutorial walkthtough Linux and Windows users through the steps of installing VS Code, the editor of choice for Rust programming. To add support for Rust syntax highlighting, code completion, and debugging to VS Code, you can install extensions like Rust Analyzer.

The building of a simple calculator program concludes the demonstration of the setup's practical application. This example not only helped you grasp the syntax and command-line operations of Rust, but it also shows you how to use external crates to make coding easier and more functional.

As an example, the clap crate is used to efficiently handle arguments passed to commands, demonstrating how simple programs may be made more powerful by utilizing Rust's extensive crate ecosystem.

As a practical exercise, this calculator program allowed you to put what you had learned into practice by parsing user input, gracefully resolving errors, and carrying out mathematical operations. It highlighted the significance of crates in Rust programming and included an example of how to integrate external libraries and manage project dependencies with Cargo.

In addition to providing you with the technical knowledge to set up your development environments, this comprehensive approach also incorporates best practices for ongoing Rust development. These include managing multiple versions of Rust and making effective use of Rust's build system and package manager to streamline workflow.

CHAPTER 3: MOST ESSENTIALS OF RUST

Introduction

This chapter explores the core concepts and elements that shape Rust into a robust and effective programming language. We will get into the concepts of shadowing and mutability in this chapter, along with the handling of variables and constants in Rust. Also covered will be the process of recognizing constants and immutable variables. As you explore the powerful capabilities of Rust functions, you will come across various types of functions, including those that utilize iterators. Building nested functions, understanding the built-in functions in Rust, and using iterators to create functions are all covered in this chapter.

In this chapter, you will learn how to use these control structures to create dynamic and responsive programs. The chapter explores more advanced aspects of Rust, like match expressions, a powerful way to deal with pattern matching, and traits, which enable the abstract definition of shared behavior. In addition, you will learn about unions and their different types, which will enhance Rust's data management capabilities.

By the end of this chapter, you will have the skills necessary to build robust applications in Rust with ease. So it's not all theory; there are coding exercises and examples to help you understand and apply the principles taught.

Variables

An essential part of data management in your programs is variables. It is not possible to change the value that has been bound to a variable because variables are inherently immutable. A fundamental feature of Rust's concurrency and safety model is its immutability, which aids in bug prevention and guarantees data consistency across various program components.

Immutable Variables

Given below is how you declare an immutable variable in Rust:

```
let x = 5;
```

In the above code snippet, **x** is bound to the value **5** and cannot be changed thereafter.

Mutable Variables

If you need a variable whose value can change, you can make it mutable by adding the **mut** keyword:

```
let mut y = 10;
```

In the above, **y** starts off with the value **10**, but it can be changed because it is mutable.

Delayed Assignment

Rust also allows you to declare a variable without immediately assigning a value to it:

```
let z;

z = 15;
```

This is useful in scenarios where the value to be assigned is not known at the point of variable declaration.

Specifying Type Annotations

While Rust is capable of inferring types in most cases, you can also explicitly specify the type of a variable:

```
let a: i32 = 20;
```

This explicitly declares **a** as an integer (i32). For mutable variables, the type can be specified in a similar manner:

```
let mut b: f64 = 3.14;
```

This declares **b** as a mutable variable of type **f64** (floating point).

Variable Shadowing

A new binding can be created in Rust by declaring a new variable with the same name as an existing one; this is called shadowing. In a limited context, this can be used to temporarily alter a variable's type or value:

```
let x = 5;

let x: f64 = x as f64;
```

In the above, **x** initially holds an integer. It is then shadowed by a new **x** that holds a floating point representation of the original value.

Another example of shadowing is changing the mutability of a variable:

```
let mut x = 5;

let x = x; // x is now immutable
```

Initially, **x** is mutable, but it is shadowed by an immutable **x**, demonstrating how shadowing can also alter mutability.

Shadowing can also be used for temporary changes:

```
let x = 10;

let x = 5;
```

This snippet shows **x** being initially set to **10**, then immediately shadowed by **5**. After the scope in which the shadowing occurs ends, **x** would revert to its original value if it is still in scope, making shadowing a versatile tool for scenarios where temporary changes are needed.

Constants

Definition

Constants are immutable values that are determined at compile-time and cannot be changed during runtime. This makes them useful for values that remain constant throughout the execution of a program, such as configuration values, scientific constants, or any other fixed values that need to be reused within the code.

To define a constant in Rust, you use the **const** keyword followed by a type annotation. Constants must always be typed because Rust needs to know how much space to allocate for them at compile time. Following is how you can define constants:

```
const MAX_POINTS: u32 = 100_000;
```

In the above code snippet, **MAX_POINTS** is a constant of type **u32** (unsigned 32-bit integer) with a value of 100,000. Constants like this are commonly used for settings or limits that do not change.

Example of Constants

Constants are particularly useful for storing scientific or commonly used numerical values. Following is how some typical constants might be defined:

```
const GRAVITATIONAL_CONSTANT: f64 = 6.674e-11;

const PI: f64 = 3.141592653589793;

const AVG_MONTHLY_RAINFALL: f32 = 3.0;

const US_POPULATION: u64 = 331_000_000;

const MAX_SPEED: u8 = 255;

const MAX_TEMPERATURE: i8 = 100;
```

Characteristics of Constants

- Unlike variables, where the compiler can often infer the type based on the assigned value, constants require explicit type annotations.

- Constants can be declared in any scope, including the global scope, which makes them useful across multiple parts of a program.

- The value of a constant must be known at compile-time, which restricts it to containing only fixed values and expressions that the compiler can evaluate.

- Using constants can be more memory-efficient than using variables, as they are not stored on the stack if they are inlined by the compiler.

Using constants can greatly improve the readability and maintainability of your code. You can ensure that a constant remains consistent across your program and that its documentation is clear by giving it a descriptive name. Because it is only needed once, there is less room for error if you ever need to change the value.

Constants Vs Immutable Variables

There is a distinction made between variables that cannot be changed and those that are constant. Defined using the **const** keyword, constants are true compile-time constants. They must be type-annotated and can only be set with a value that is known at compile time. Constants are ideal for defining values that are used across multiple parts of a program and don't change. They must be declared in a global scope, which makes them accessible throughout the program, but they cannot be declared inside functions.

```
const MAX_POINTS: u32 = 100_000; // Constant declaration
```

On the other hand, immutable variables are declared with the **let** keyword and their immutability simply means they cannot be reassigned after their initial assignment. Unlike constants, they do not need to be globally scoped and can be declared within functions. The Rust compiler can often infer the type of these variables from the initial assignment, so explicit type annotation isn't necessary. Immutable variables can also be shadowed, which means you can declare a new variable with the same name that can optionally have a different type or value.

```rust
let current_points = 50_000; // Immutable variable

let current_points = 75_000; // Shadowing the previous
immutable variable
```

Sample Program

Given below is a practical example to illustrate the use of constants and immutable variables within a Rust program:

```rust
fn main() {

 // Constant: Global and fixed compile-time value with
explicit type

 const MAX_POINTS: u32 = 100_000;

 println!("Maximum points allowed: {}", MAX_POINTS);


 // Immutable variable: Local and can be shadowed

 let current_points = 50_000;

 println!("Current points: {}", current_points);


 // Shadowing the immutable variable with a new value

 let current_points = 75_000;
```

```
 println!("Updated points after shadowing: {}",
current_points);


 // Attempting to reassign either will cause a compile-
time error

 // Uncommenting either line below will result in a
compiler error

 // MAX_POINTS = 120_000; // Error: cannot assign twice
to immutable variable

 // current_points = 100_000; // Error: cannot assign
twice to immutable variable

}
```

This code clearly defines how constants and immutable variables behave differently in terms of scope, reassignment, and type requirements. Constants are fixed and unchangeable once defined and are used for values that truly are constant throughout the application. Immutable variables, while not reassignable, can be shadowed within their scope, providing flexibility in scenarios such as looping constructs or conditional branches where reusing a variable name for a new value is beneficial.

Following is an example that illustrates the difference between constants and immutable variables:

```
fn main() {

 // This constant is defined using the `const` keyword
and must have a type specified.

 // Constants are evaluated at compile time and must be
immutable.

 const PI: f64 = 3.141592653589793;
```

```rust
// Immutable variable defined with `let`. Rust can often
infer the type from the assigned value.

// Immutable variables can be declared inside functions
and do not have to be global.

let radius = 2.0;


// Attempting to modify the constant `PI` would result
in a compile-time error.

// Uncommenting the following line will cause a compiler
error:

// PI = 3.14; // Error: cannot assign twice to immutable
variable `PI`


// The immutable variable `radius` cannot be modified
once it is assigned.

// The following line, if uncommented, will also produce
a compile-time error:

// radius = 2.5; // Error: cannot assign twice to
immutable variable `radius`


// However, Rust allows shadowing of the `radius`
variable by using the same name within the same function.

// This does not change the original `radius` but
creates a new variable with the same name.

let radius = 2.5;
```

```
println!("The value of PI is approximately {}", PI);

println!("The new value of radius is {}", radius);

}
```

In this script:

- **PI** is a constant representing the mathematical constant pi, crucial for calculations involving circles. It's precisely defined with a type **f64** and cannot be changed once set.

- **radius** starts as an immutable variable set to **2.0**. It demonstrates immutability by being unable to be directly reassigned but shows how Rust allows for reassignment through shadowing, where **radius** is redeclared with a new value of **2.5**.

Shadowing Vs Mutability

Shadowing and mutability are two distinct features that handle variable values in different ways, each with its own use case depending on the desired behavior in your code.

Shadowing

Shadowing allows you to declare a new variable with the same name as a previous variable. The new variable effectively "shadows" the old variable within its scope, which means the original variable remains unchanged and inaccessible unless the shadowing scope ends. This feature is particularly useful when you need to transform the type of a variable or start with a new value while retaining the immutability of the original variable. Following is how you can use shadowing:

```
fn main() {

 let x = 5; // Immutable variable

 let x = x + 5; // Shadowing `x` with a new value


 println!("x = {}", x); // prints "x = 10"

}
```

In the above code snippet, **x** is first initialized to **5**. Then, it is shadowed by a new **x** which is the result of **x + 5**. This new **x** does not affect the original **x** outside of its scope.

Mutability

Mutability, on the other hand, allows you to change the value of a variable directly after its initial assignment. This is done by declaring a variable with the **mut** keyword, which makes the variable mutable. Mutable variables are useful when a variable's value needs to be updated without the overhead of creating a new variable:

```
fn main() {

  let mut y = 5; // Mutable variable

  y = y + 5; // Directly modifying `y`


  println!("y = {}", y); // prints "y = 10"

}
```

In the above, **y** starts with a value of **5** and is then directly modified to **10** by adding **5** to the original value. The **mut** keyword is essential as it allows direct modification.

Choosing Between Shadowing and Mutability

The choice between shadowing and mutability depends on your specific needs:

- Shadowing is used when you need to overwrite a variable to use it for a new purpose or in a changed form while maintaining the original variable's immutability. It's also useful for changing the type of the variable.

- Mutability is more straightforward when you simply need to update or change the variable's value multiple times.

Functions

In Rust, a function is defined with the **fn** keyword, followed by a name, a set of parameters, and, optionally, a return type. The body of the function is enclosed in braces **{}**. Given below is an example of a simple function:

```
fn add(x: i32, y: i32) -> i32 {

  x + y

}
```

This function, named **add**, takes two parameters, **x** and **y**, both of which are of type **i32** (a 32-bit signed integer). It returns their sum, also as an **i32**. The return type of the function is specified after the **->** symbol. In this case, the function's body contains a single expression **x + y** which automatically becomes the return value.

To use this function within your Rust program, you would call it by passing the required parameters. For example:

```
let sum = add(5, 10);
```

This call computes the sum of 5 and 10 using the **add** function and assigns the result (**15**) to the variable **sum**.

Functions can handle more complex scenarios, including taking more complex types as arguments or containing more logic within their body. For instance, consider a function that determines the longest string in a vector of strings:

```
fn longest_string(strings: Vec<String>) -> String {

  let mut longest = strings[0].clone();

  for s in &strings {

  if s.len() > longest.len() {

  longest = s.clone();

  }

  }

  longest

}
```

This function, **longest_string**, takes a vector of **String** objects and returns the longest string. It uses iteration and conditional logic to find the longest string by comparing the length of each string with the current longest string. The above code snippet demonstrates how functions can encapsulate more complex logic, making your code more organized and reusable.

Types of Functions

Rust offers a versatile approach to defining functions, accommodating different programming paradigms and styles. This flexibility is demonstrated through the various types of functions you can define and use in Rust, each serving distinct purposes and use cases.

Free Functions

These are the standard functions that you declare using the **fn** keyword. They do not belong to any object or struct and are accessible from anywhere within the scope they are declared in. Given below is an example of a free function that adds two integers:

```
fn add(x: i32, y: i32) -> i32 {

  x + y

}
```

Method Functions

Methods are functions tied to a struct or an enum. They are defined within an **impl** block for the type they relate to and can access the data of the struct or enum instances via the **self** keyword. Following is how you can define a method for a **Point** struct that calculates the distance from the origin:

```
struct Point {

  x: i32,

  y: i32,

}
```

```
impl Point {

 fn distance_from_origin(&self) -> f64 {

  ((self.x.pow(2) + self.y.pow(2)) as f64).sqrt()

 }
```

Closure Functions

Closures are anonymous functions that can capture variables from their surrounding environment. They are defined using pipes || that contain their parameters and can be stored in variables or passed around as arguments. Given below is an example of a closure that adds two to its input:

```
let add_two = |x: i32| x + 2;
```

Generator Functions

Although not officially supported as a distinct function type like in some other languages, Rust can mimic generator-like behavior using iterators. Given below is a simple example of a function that returns an iterator starting from a given integer:

```
fn count_up_from(start: i32) -> impl Iterator<Item = i32>
{

 (start..)

}
```

In the main function, these types are utilized as follows:

```
fn main() {

 // Free function usage

 println!("The sum of 3 and 4 is {}", add(3, 4));
```

```
// Method function usage

let point = Point { x: 5, y: 10 };

println!("The distance from the origin is {}",
point.distance_from_origin());


// Closure function usage

println!("3 plus 2 is {}", add_two(3));


// Using the generator function

let mut generator = count_up_from(5);

println!("{}", generator.next().unwrap()); // Prints 5

println!("{}", generator.next().unwrap()); // Prints 6

}
```

Each function type caters to specific needs: free functions for general procedures, methods for object-oriented style encapsulation, closures for functional programming and flexibility, and generator-like functions for creating sequences or streams of data.

Writing a Rust Function

You can define a function using the **fn** keyword, followed by the function's name, parameters, and return type. The function body is enclosed in curly braces **{}**. Given below is a simple function that takes an integer **x** and returns its square:

```
fn square(x: i32) -> i32 {

x * x
```

```
}
```

This function is named **square**, takes one parameter **x** of type **i32** (a 32-bit integer), and returns an **i32**. The operation **x * x** computes the square of **x**, and since there are no explicit return statements, Rust returns the last expression implicitly.

Calling the Function

To use this function within your Rust program, you simply call it by passing the required argument. Following is how you can call this function:

```
let y = square(5);
```

This line calls the **square** function with **5** as an argument and stores the result in a variable **y**. Since **5 * 5 = 25**, the variable **y** will hold the value **25**.

Combining these concepts, following is a complete Rust program that defines and calls the **square** function:

```
fn main() {

 let x = 5;

 let y = square(x);

 println!("The square of {} is {}", x, y);

}



fn square(x: i32) -> i32 {

 x * x

}
```

This program defines a **main** function where it initializes a variable **x** with the value **5**, calls the **square** function to compute the square of **x**, and stores the result in **y**. It then prints out the result using **println!**, a macro to print output to the console.

When you run this program, it will output:

```
The square of 5 is 25
```

The above code snippet illustrates the basic structure of a Rust program with a custom function.

Coding a Function with an Iterator

An iterator is any type that implements the **Iterator** trait. This trait requires the implementation of a method **.next()**, which returns an **Option** that is either **Some(item)** if there is another item in the sequence, or **None** if all items have been iterated over. Iterators are powerful because they allow for lazy evaluation; they compute their items as they are needed.

Sample Program: Summing Values with an Iterator

Given below is an example of a Rust function that sums integers from an iterator:

```
fn sum_iterator<I: Iterator<Item = i32>>(iter: I) -> i32
{

  iter.fold(0, |acc, x| acc + x)

}
```

This function, **sum_iterator**, takes an iterator over items of type **i32** as its input and uses the **fold** method to accumulate a sum. The **fold** method takes two parameters: an initial accumulator value (**0** in this case) and a closure that describes how to combine the accumulator and an element of the iterator (**acc + x**).

To utilize this function, you can pass it an iterator. For example, you might want to sum the values in a vector:

```
let v = vec![1, 2, 3, 4];

let result = sum_iterator(v.into_iter());

println!("The sum is: {}", result);
```

In this snippet:

- **`vec![1, 2, 3, 4]`** creates a vector containing the integers 1 through 4.

- **`v.into_iter()`** converts the vector into an iterator.

- **`sum_iterator(v.into_iter())`** calls the summing function with the iterator.

When run, this code outputs: "The sum is: 10", as it sums the elements 1, 2, 3, and 4. By leveraging iterators, you can write more generic, reusable functions that work with any data type that can be iterated over, not just collections like arrays or vectors.

Passing Function As Arguments

Function as Arguments

You can pass functions as arguments by specifying the function's signature as the argument's type. This involves stating the types of the function's parameters and its return type. Given below is how you can define and use such functionality:

```rust
fn apply_twice<F>(f: F, x: i32) -> i32

 where F: Fn(i32) -> i32

{

 f(f(x))

}
```

In the above coded snippet,

- **`apply_twice`** is a function that takes two parameters: **f** and **x**.

- **F** is a generic type parameter for the function argument **f**, which is bound by the trait **`Fn(i32) -> i32`**. This means **f** must be a function (or a closure) that takes a single **i32** argument and returns an **i32**.

- Inside **`apply_twice`**, the function **f** is called twice on **x**: first **`f(x)`** is evaluated, and then **f** is called again on the result of the first call.

Using Function

To utilize this function with a specific operation, define a closure that matches the required signature and pass it to **`apply_twice`**. Given below is an example:

```
let double = |x| x * 2;

let y = apply_twice(double, 5);
```

In this case:

- **double** is a closure that takes an integer, doubles it, and returns the result.

- **y** will hold the result of applying **double** twice to **5**. Thus, **double(5)** results in **10**, and **double(10)** results in **20**.

- The final value of **y** is **20**, which demonstrates the closure being applied twice.

Nested Function (Function Within Function)

Overview

A nested function is defined directly inside another function. It can access the outer function's variables and parameters, which can be particularly useful for operations that require several steps of processing that are only relevant within a single outer function.

Sample Program

Given below is an example to illustrate how nested functions can be implemented and utilized in Rust:

```
fn outer(x: i32) -> i32 {

 // Define a nested function

 fn inner(y: i32) -> i32 {

 y * 2 // Simple operation that doubles the input

 }


 inner(x) // Call the nested function with the outer
function's parameter
```

```
}

fn main() {

  let input = 5;

  let result = outer(input);

  println!("The result is {}", result); // Outputs: The
result is 10

}
```

In the above sample program,

- **outer** is a function that takes an integer **x**.
- **inner** is a nested function defined within **outer** that doubles its input.
- **outer** calls **inner**, passing **x** to it, and returns the result.
- The main function demonstrates calling **outer** with an argument of **5**, which results in an output of **10** after **inner** processes it.

This structure is particularly useful when **inner** performs a task that is only relevant in the context of what **outer** is designed to achieve, helping to encapsulate functionality and reduce the complexity of the code outside of **outer**.

Built-In Functions

Overview

Whether you are dealing with basic input/output operations or more advanced thread management or network communications, Rust's extensive standard library has you covered with a plethora of built-in functions and macros. The development of reliable and efficient applications is impossible without these tools.

Built-In Functions/Macros In Use

- **println!** and **print!**: These macros are used for printing output to the console. **println!** adds a newline after the message, whereas **print!** does not.

- **format!**: This macro is used to format strings. It works similarly to **println!**, but instead of printing the result, it returns a **String** with the formatted text.

- File operations (**std::fs**):
  - **read_to_string**: Reads the contents of a file into a **String**.
  - **write_all**: Writes data to a file, typically used through a **File** instance.

- Thread management (**std::thread**):
  - **spawn**: Used to create a new thread.
  - **sleep**: Pauses the current thread for a specified duration.

- Networking (**std::net**):
  - **TcpStream::connect**: Establishes a TCP connection to a specified address.

- Collection utilities:
  - **vec!**: A macro to create a new vector populated with specified elements.
  - **String::new**: Creates a new, empty **String**.
  - **String::push_str**: Appends a string slice onto the end of a **String**.
  - **str::split**: Splits a string into an iterator of substrings according to a delimiter.
  - **slice::join**: Combines a slice of strings into a single string with a specified separator.

- Hash map operations (**std::collections::HashMap**):
  - **new**: Creates a new, empty hash map.
  - **insert**: Adds a key-value pair to the hash map.
  - **get**: Retrieves a reference to the value corresponding to the key in the hash map.

- Error handling:
  - **result::unwrap**: Unwraps a **Result** type, yielding the contained **Ok** value, or panicking if it's an **Err**.

Sample Program

Following is how you might see some of these functions used in a simple Rust program:

```rust
use std::fs;

use std::thread;

use std::time::Duration;


fn main() {
 // Print and format a greeting

 let name = "Alice";

 println!("Hello, {}", name);


 // Read from a file

 let data = fs::read_to_string("data.txt").expect("Unable
to read file");


 // Spawn a new thread and sleep

 thread::spawn(|| {

 thread::sleep(Duration::from_millis(100));

 println!("Thread awake!");

 });


 // Working with collections

 let mut vec = vec![1, 2, 3];
```

```
vec.push(4);

println!("{:?}", vec);
```

}This snippet demonstrates reading a file, managing threads, and utilizing vectors, showing just a few of the powerful utilities available in Rust's standard library.

If Statements

Overview

The **if** statement is a fundamental control flow structure that allows you to branch your code based on conditions. Using **if**, **else if**, and **else**, you can execute different blocks of code depending on the truth value of boolean expressions.

Sample Program

Given below is a practical example to illustrate how you can use **if** statements in Rust, particularly with input that varies, such as random numbers:

```
use rand::Rng; // Import the Rng trait from the rand
crate


fn main() {

  let mut rng = rand::thread_rng(); // Create a random
number generator

  let n = rng.gen_range(-5..5); // Generate a random
number between -5 and 4


  if n < 0 {

  println!("negative value"); // Executes if n is less
than 0
```

```
} else if n == 0 {

println!("zero"); // Executes if n is exactly 0

} else {

println!("positive value"); // Executes if n is greater
than 0

}

}
```

How It Works?

Random Number Generation
- **rand::thread_rng()** provides a local random number generator.
- **rng.gen_range(-5..5)** generates a random integer within the specified range (note: the upper bound is exclusive).

Conditional Branching
- The **if** statement checks if **n** is less than 0. If this condition is true, it prints "negative value."
- The **else if** follows up by checking if **n** is exactly 0, only evaluating this condition if the first **if** was false.
- Finally, the **else** block covers all other cases not handled by the preceding conditions, in this case when **n** is positive.

Execution Flow

- Only one block among the **if**, **else if**, and **else** will execute based on the value of **n**.
- This setup ensures that your program can appropriately handle different cases with a clear and understandable structure.

The above sample program demonstrates how to use branching logic in Rust in a simple way, illustrating how conditional statements can handle flow control with dynamic data. This is especially helpful in programs that need to make decisions based on user data, file contents, or random numbers, as demonstrated in the above sample program.

Loop Statements

Overview

The **loop** keyword is used to create an infinite loop that will keep executing the block of code inside it until it explicitly encounters a **break** statement. This looping mechanism is powerful for situations where you need to keep running a block of code until a certain condition is met.

Sample Program

Given below is a revised example that uses the **loop** statement to repeatedly print a message until a condition is fulfilled:

```
fn main() {

 let mut i = 0; // Counter variable initialized


 loop {

 println!("falcon"); // Action to repeat


 i += 1; // Increment the counter

 if i == 5 { // Condition to exit the loop

 break; // Exit the loop

 }

 }

}
```

In the above sample program,

- **let mut i = 0;** starts a counter at 0. The **mut** keyword is necessary because the value of **i** will change as the loop progresses.

- The **loop** keyword begins an infinite loop. Everything inside the curly braces **{}** will execute repeatedly until a **break** is encountered.

- **println!("falcon");** is the action performed in each iteration of the loop. In this case, it prints the word "falcon" to the console.

- Each time the loop executes, the counter **i** is incremented by 1 (**i += 1;**). The **if i == 5** statement checks if **i** has reached 5. If true, the **break** statement terminates the loop.

- The **break** keyword immediately exits the loop, and any code following the loop (not shown here) will then execute.

The **loop** statement is particularly useful in scenarios where the number of iterations is not known in advance or when waiting for a specific event to occur, such as receiving user input or a file becoming available. It's a fundamental part of creating robust, interactive, and responsive applications in Rust.

While Statements

Overview

The **while** statement creates a loop that continues executing as long as a specified condition remains true. This loop is particularly useful for performing repeated actions where the number of iterations is not known before the loop begins, but a condition to end the loop is clearly defined.

Sample Program

Let us take a detailed look at how to use the **while** loop with two practical examples:

Example 1: Counting from 1 to 10

In the first example, we use a **while** loop to print numbers from 1 through 10. This simple loop demonstrates how to implement a counter that increments on each iteration until it reaches a certain condition.

```
fn main() {

  let mut x = 1;
```

```
while x <= 10 {

println!("{}", x);

x += 1;

}


println!("x: {}", x); // Outputs the final value of x
after the loop ends

}
```

In this code:

- **x** is initialized to 1.

- The **while** loop checks if **x** is less than or equal to 10.

- Inside the loop, **x** is printed and then incremented by 1.

- After exiting the loop, the final value of **x** is printed, which will be 11, showing that the loop has completed its execution because the condition **x <= 10** is no longer true.

Example 2: Calculating the Sum of a Vector

The second example calculates the sum of integers stored in a vector. This demonstrates how **while** loops can be used to iterate over array-like structures when the number of iterations depends on the size of the data structure.

```
fn main() {

let vals = vec![1, 2, 3, 4, 5, 6, 7, 8, 9, 10]; // A
vector of integers


let mut i = 0; // Index for the vector
```

```
let mut sum = 0; // Variable to store the sum

let n = vals.len(); // The number of elements in the
vector


while i < n {

sum += vals[i];

i += 1;

}


println!("The sum is: {}", sum); // Outputs the sum of
the vector

}
```

In the above sample program,

- We initialize a vector **vals** with integers from 1 to 10.

- **i** is used as an index to access elements in the vector, starting from 0.

- **sum** accumulates the sum of the elements.

- The **while** loop continues until **i** is less than the length of the vector (**n**).

- On each iteration, the current element **vals[i]** is added to **sum**, and **i** is incremented.

Key Points

1. The **while** loop is ideal for scenarios where the loop must continue until a condition changes, often used for looping over data or waiting for a state change.

2. Unlike **for** loops, **while** loops do not inherently know about the structure they are iterating over, and thus require explicit management of the loop variable and condition.

For Statements

Overview

The **for** statement is a powerful tool for iterating over sequences like ranges and collections. It is used extensively for its clarity and efficiency, especially when dealing with elements in an array or executing a block of code a specific number of times.

Sample Program: Iterate through Range

Given below is a simple example of using a **for** loop to iterate over a range from 1 to 10, inclusive:

```
fn main() {

 // Iterating over a range from 1 to 10

 for i in 1..=10 {

 print!("{} ", i);

 }

 println!(); // Prints a newline after the loop

}
```

In the above sample program, **for i in 1..=10** iterates over numbers from 1 to 10. The **..=** syntax is used to make the range inclusive of the upper bound, meaning **10** is included in the loop. Each number is printed on the same line, separated by spaces.

Sample Program: Iterating Over an Array

The **for** loop is also highly effective for iterating through arrays. Given below is how you might use it to iterate over an array of integers:

```
fn main() {

 let vals = [1, 2, 3, 4, 5, 6, 7, 8, 9, 10]; // Array of
integers
```

```
// Iterating over each element in the array

for e in vals {

print!("{} ", e);

}

println!(); // Prints a newline after the loop

}
```

In this snippet, **vals** is an array of integers. The loop **for e in vals** goes through each element in the array **vals**, assigning it to **e** and then executing the body of the loop which prints each element. This demonstrates the **for** loop's ability to handle collections such as arrays efficiently.

Advantages

- The **for** loop syntax is straightforward, making your code easy to read and understand. It explicitly states the variable being used for iteration and the collection or range being iterated over.

- Iterating with a **for** loop is safe because it handles the bounds of the collection automatically, reducing errors like off-by-one or accessing invalid indices.

- You can iterate over anything that implements the **Iterator** trait, not just ranges or arrays but also other collections like **Vec**, **HashMap**, or even custom data structures.

Match Expression

Overview

The **match** expression is an extremely versatile and powerful tool for control flow, allowing values to be compared against patterns and different actions to be taken based on which pattern matches. This form of pattern matching is particularly useful for handling various possible cases in a concise and clear manner.

Sample Program

In a **match** statement, each potential case is an "arm," which consists of a pattern and the code that should be executed if the value given to **match** fits that pattern. Given below is how it can be effectively utilized:

```
fn main() {

 let grades = ["A", "B", "C", "D", "E", "F", "FX"];


 for grade in grades {

 match grade {

 "A" | "B" | "C" | "D" | "E" | "F" => println!("passed"),

 "FX" => println!("failed"),

 _ => println!("unknown"), // Catch-all for unexpected
values

 }

 }

}
```

In the above sample program,

- **grades** is an array containing strings representing different grades.
- A **for** loop is used to iterate through each grade in the array.
- For each grade, **match** checks which pattern the grade conforms to.
- Multiple patterns (e.g., **"A" | "B" | "C"**...) are combined using the **|** operator, which is useful when multiple patterns lead to the same outcome.
- The **"FX"** grade has its own arm, printing **"failed"**.
- The underscore _ acts as a catch-all pattern that matches any value, handling unexpected or unknown grades by printing **"unknown"**.

Advantages

- The **match** expression makes it clear what the possible outcomes are for each case, reducing the risk of unexpected behavior that can arise with more verbose conditional logic like a series of **if**/**else** statements.

- Rust's compiler checks to ensure every possible case is handled or explicitly ignored; this is particularly useful in ensuring that no case is accidentally overlooked.

- **match** can handle not just equality checks but also more complex pattern matching against data structures, enums, and ranges.

Match offers an organized and efficient way to run separate blocks of code depending on a variable's value by concatenating multiple grades and differentiating only when needed.

Traits Basics

Overview

Traits are a powerful feature used to define shared behavior in an abstract way. They are similar to interfaces in other languages but offer more flexibility, allowing you to specify not only the methods a type must implement but also the type of the arguments and return values of those methods.

Working of Traits

Given below is a fundamental example to illustrate how traits work in Rust:

```
// Definition of a trait named Eq

trait Eq {

  fn eq(&self, other: &Self) -> bool;

}



// Implementing the trait for the i32 type

impl Eq for i32 {
```

```
fn eq(&self, other: &i32) -> bool {

*self == *other

}

}
```

In the above code snippet,

- The **Eq** trait defines a method **eq** that checks equality between two references to the same type (**Self**). This method returns a **bool**.

- The implementation of **Eq** for the type **i32** uses simple equality checking. It allows an **i32** instance to compare itself with another **i32**.

Trait Usage

With the trait implemented, you can now use the **eq** method on instances of **i32**:

```
let x = 5;

let y = 10;

assert!(x.eq(&y) == false);
```

In the above code snippet, **x.eq(&y)** checks if **x** is equal to **y** and returns **false** since 5 is not equal to 10.

Advantages

- Traits allow you to define common behaviors that multiple types can implement, promoting code reuse and reducing duplication.

- By defining a trait, you can write functions and methods that operate on any type that implements the trait, without knowing the specifics of how each type behaves.

- Traits ensure that only appropriate methods are called on types that can handle them, enhancing type safety and reducing errors.

- Traits can be used with dynamic dispatch to call methods on types determined at runtime, offering flexibility in how objects are handled.

Sample Program: Traits for Dynamic Dispatch

To use traits for dynamic dispatch, you can define methods that accept trait objects. Given below is a simple demonstration:

```
fn print_equality<T: Eq>(a: &T, b: &T) {

  println!("Are they equal? {}", a.eq(b));

}



print_equality(&5, &5); // Outputs: Are they equal? true
```

This function **print_equality** accepts any type **T** that implements the **Eq** trait and checks if two references are equal using the **eq** method defined by the trait.

Types of Traits

You can create code that is more versatile and easier to reuse if you have a good grasp of the various traits. A few important kinds of traits in Rust are listed below, with examples for each:

Basic Traits

These are standard traits that define methods to be implemented by types. An example is a trait for displaying an object:

```
trait Display {

  fn display(&self) -> String;

}



struct Person {

  name: String,

  age: u32,
```

```
}
```

```
impl Display for Person {

  fn display(&self) -> String {

  format!("{} ({})", self.name, self.age)

  }

}
```

```
let person = Person { name: "Alice".to_string(), age: 30
};

println!("{}", person.display());
```

This **Display** trait defines a method for returning a string representation of a type, similar to the built-in **std::fmt::Display**.

Marker Traits

Marker traits convey metadata about a type and do not require any methods. A common example is the **Copy** trait, which indicates that a type's instances can be duplicated by simple bitwise copying:

```
trait Copy {}


struct Point {

  x: i32,

  y: i32,

}
```

```
impl Copy for Point {}
```

In the above, **Point** is marked with the **Copy** trait, suggesting that it can be copied cheaply. No methods are defined or needed for this trait.

Generic Traits with Associated Types

These traits allow types to carry associated types with them, providing a way to define generic containers or interfaces:

```
trait Container {

  type Item;

  fn get(&self, index: usize) -> Option<&Self::Item>;

}



struct List<T> {

  elements: Vec<T>,

}



impl<T> Container for List<T> {

  type Item = T;


  fn get(&self, index: usize) -> Option<&T> {

  self.elements.get(index)

  }
```

```
}
```

In the above code snippet, **Container** is a generic trait with an associated type **Item**. It's implemented for a struct **List**, with **Item** being the type of elements in the list.

Operator Overloading Traits

Rust allows you to overload certain operators for custom types using specific traits:

```
use std::ops::Add;


struct Matrix {

  elements: Vec<Vec<i32>>,

}


impl Add for Matrix {

  type Output = Matrix;


  fn add(self, other: Matrix) -> Matrix {

  let mut result = self.elements.clone();


  for (i, row) in self.elements.iter().enumerate() {

  for (j, &val) in row.iter().enumerate() {

  result[i][j] += other.elements[i][j];

  }
```

```
    }

    Matrix { elements: result }

    }

}
```

This **Add** trait implementation allows two matrices to be added together, returning a new **Matrix**.

Trait Objects for Dynamic Dispatch

When you need runtime polymorphism, you can use trait objects. Given below is a quick example:

```
trait Animal {

  fn speak(&self);

}


struct Dog;

struct Cat;


impl Animal for Dog {

  fn speak(&self) {

  println!("Woof!");

  }

}
```

```
impl Animal for Cat {

 fn speak(&self) {

 println!("Meow!");

 }

}


let animals: Vec<Box<dyn Animal>> = vec![Box::new(Dog),
Box::new(Cat)];

for animal in animals {

 animal.speak();

}
```

This setup with **Animal** trait and its implementations for **Dog** and **Cat** use dynamic dispatch to call the appropriate **speak** method at runtime based on the actual type of the object.

Do's and Don'ts

Do's of Traits

Define Common Behaviors

Use traits to encapsulate common behaviors that multiple types can share. This approach promotes code reuse and interface consistency.

Utilize Associated Types

When defining a trait, use associated types to introduce placeholders that can be specified later when implementing the trait. This allows for greater flexibility and type safety in trait methods.

Specify Type Bounds

Use type bounds to enforce that generics must implement certain traits, thus ensuring that the generic types behave as expected.

Implement Traits with impl

Use the **impl** keyword to provide specific implementations of the traits for your types, allowing you to customize behavior per type.

Don'ts of Trait

Overuse Single-Method Traits

Avoid defining traits with only one method unless it provides significant abstraction benefit. Instead, consider using simpler alternatives like function pointers or closures if a single method is all you need.

Misuse Traits as Types

Do not use traits directly as types in places like struct fields or standalone variables. Instead, use specific types that implement these traits or use trait objects where dynamic dispatch is necessary.

Inappropriately Use Traits in Function Signatures

While it's common to use traits in function parameters or return types for polymorphism, ensure that it's done wisely to avoid overly generic interfaces that can obscure a function's purpose. Use concrete types or bounded generics to clarify your API.

Avoid Mutable Methods in Traits

Be cautious when adding methods that take mutable references to **self** in traits. This can complicate the usage of your trait, especially in concurrent contexts. Immutable methods are generally easier to manage and reason about.

Sample Program: Using Traits Effectively

Given below is a revised example based on the above given do's and don'ts:

```
trait Drawable {

  fn draw(&self); // Immutable reference, suitable for
read-only operations

}
```

```rust
struct Circle {
  radius: f32,
}


struct Square {
  side: f32,
}


impl Drawable for Circle {
  fn draw(&self) {
  println!("Drawing a circle with radius: {}",
self.radius);
  }
}


impl Drawable for Square {
  fn draw(&self) {
  println!("Drawing a square with side: {}", self.side);
  }
}
```

```rust
fn display_shape(shape: &impl Drawable) {

  shape.draw();

}


fn main() {

  let circle = Circle { radius: 5.0 };

  let square = Square { side: 10.0 };


  display_shape(&circle);

  display_shape(&square);

}
```

In the above sample program,

- The **Drawable** trait is used to define a common behavior **draw**, which is implemented by multiple types (**Circle** and **Square**).

- Implementation uses the **impl** keyword to define behavior specific to each type.

- The trait methods use an immutable reference to **self**, avoiding potential issues with mutable state management.

- A function **display_shape** uses a trait bound to accept any type that implements **Drawable**, demonstrating polymorphism without compromising function clarity.

Unions

A union is a sophisticated data structure that permits numerous fields to share a single memory location. When there are several possible representations of a value, but only one is actually used at any given time, they are helpful for memory-efficient storage. Familiarity with Rust's memory safety principles, especially **unsafe** blocks, is necessary for comprehending the proper and secure use of unions.

Defining Unions

Given below is an example that illustrates how to define and use unions in Rust:

```rust
// Define a union with i32 and f32 types

union MyUnion {

 i: i32,

 f: f32,

}


fn main() {

 let mut u = MyUnion { i: 10 }; // Initialize the union with an integer


 unsafe {

 // Accessing a union's field is unsafe

 println!("u.i = {}", u.i); // Safe to access because it's the last value written

 u.f = 3.14; // Reassign to store a float

 println!("u.f = {}", u.f); // Now safe to access f

 }

}
```

In the above code snippet, **MyUnion** can store either an **i32** or an **f32**, but only one at a time. Access to union fields must be wrapped in an **unsafe** block because Rust cannot guarantee type safety at compile time for unions.

Types of Unions

Unions can contain a variety of field types, each with specific use cases:

Enumerations

```
enum Color {

  Red,

  Green,

  Blue,

}


union MyUnion {

  c: Color,

  i: i32,

}
```

Structs

```
struct Point {

  x: i32,

  y: i32,

}
```

```
union MyUnion {

 p: Point,

 i: i32,

}
```

Arrays

```
union MyUnion {

 a: [i32; 4],

 i: i32,

}
```

Because of the importance of managing type safety when working with unions—especially in concurrent contexts where data races are possible—field access to unions is encapsulated in **unsafe** blocks to guarantee that only the correct field is accessed at any one time.

Implementing Unions

Following is a detailed, easy-to-follow instruction on how to make use of unions in Rust.

Define the Union

First, define a union using the **union** keyword. The union can include fields of various types, but all fields share the same memory space. Given below is an example using primitive types:

```
union MyUnion {

 i: i32,

 f: f32,

}
```

This definition creates a union called **MyUnion** with two fields: **i** of type **i32** and **f** of type **f32**. The union will allocate enough memory to hold the largest of its fields, in this case, both are the same size.

Create an Instance

You can instantiate a union by specifying a value for one of its fields. Given below is how you might initialize it:

```
let mut u = MyUnion { i: 10 };
```

This initializes **u** with the **i** field set to **10**. Do not forget that even though you set one field, the union shares the same space for all fields.

Access the Union Fields

Accessing fields of a union is unsafe because Rust cannot guarantee that the correct data type is being read – it might lead to undefined behavior. Accessing union data must therefore be enclosed in **unsafe** blocks:

```
unsafe {

  println!("u.i = {}", u.i);

}
```

This code safely prints the value of the **i** field. Remember, safety is the programmer's responsibility in these blocks.

Modify the Fields

You can also modify the fields of the union, but like reading, writing to a union is unsafe and must be done within an **unsafe** block:

```
unsafe {

  u.f = 3.14;

  println!("u.f = {}", u.f);

}
```

After assigning a new value to the **f** field, the above code prints the new value of **f**. This operation overwrites the data that was in **i**, demonstrating how unions can hold different data types in the same memory location.

Implementation Summary

Combining all these steps, given below is a complete program using a union:

```
union MyUnion {

  i: i32,

  f: f32,

}


fn main() {

  let mut u = MyUnion { i: 10 };


  unsafe {

  println!("u.i = {}", u.i);

  u.f = 3.14;

  println!("u.f = {}", u.f);

  }

}
```

The output is as below:

```
u.i = 10

u.f = 3.14
```

Please do remember that using unions involves careful consideration of how data is managed in memory. Incorrect usage can lead to hard-to-find bugs. It's important to use **unsafe** code judiciously and ensure that any operations within **unsafe** blocks maintain memory safety.

Summary

Central to grasping and making good use of the language are the basic ideas covered in this chapter. We began with variables, going over their declaration and initialization processes while drawing attention to the distinction between immutable and mutable variables. Constants, which are like variables but don't change value once defined, were also covered in the chapter.

With the introduction of shadowing, variables could be renamed to reflect new types or values while still remaining in the same scope; this allowed for the reuse of the names without altering the original variables. Also demonstrated were the fundamentals and advanced features of Rust's functions, including their definition, passing of arguments, return of values, and the use of traits for function overloading.

We covered control flow constructs like while, for, and loop, which allow code to be executed repeatedly under specific conditions or based on conditions, as well as if-else statements. Match expressions, taught in the chapter as a more robust and versatile substitute for switch statements in other languages, were also covered in depth, allowing for pattern matching against values.

The chapter also introduced the useful idea of traits, a way to characterize commonalities in behavior across types. The usage of traits allows for the implementation of shared functionality across various structs or enums.

Additionally, unions were highlighted as a data structure that can store data in various forms. Their usefulness in low-level systems programming, where memory efficiency is paramount, was emphasized. Since accessing union data necessitates unsafe code blocks, safety precautions were brought up in the union topic, mirroring Rust's focus on memory safety.

CHAPTER 4: STRUCTS

Introduction

Building strong and maintainable applications is the goal of every Rust developer, and this chapter looks into the fundamental and flexible topic of structs in Rust. With the help of structures, you can easily organize and manage your code by grouping related data together.

The fundamentals of structs and their role in Rust's architecture will be covered first. Here you will find an introduction to various structs, including tuple structs, classic C-style structs, and unit structs, all of which have their own specific uses in programming.

Now we'll get into the meat of the chapter, which is teaching you how to write programs with structs. Both fundamental and advanced methods, such as custom struct definitions, will be required for this. You can customize data structures to meet the specific needs of your projects with the help of custom structs, which give you greater control and flexibility over your data.

Structs within structs, or nested structs, will also be covered. Building complicated data structures that more closely resemble real-world data is made easier with this idea. Another thing you'll learn is how to use traits and type composition to mimic struct inheritance patterns. This is a powerful way to reuse code without the pitfalls of classical inheritance, even though Rust doesn't support traditional class-based inheritance.

The chapter will conclude with an understanding of the dos and don'ts of struct usage in Rust. You should feel confident using structs in a variety of contexts by the time you finish this chapter, from defining basic data containers to implementing complex, custom-typed data structures designed for advanced software systems.

Understanding Structs

Definition and Usage

Structs are fundamental building blocks for organizing data. They let you group related data items together under one name in a way that makes it easier to manage and understand your code. Structs are especially useful when modeling complex entities and serve as the foundation for custom data types that represent various concepts in a program.

Following is a sample program of how structs work while developing Rust applications:

```
// Define a simple struct with two fields

struct Point {

  x: i32,
```

```rust
  y: i32,

}


// Create an instance of the struct

let p = Point { x: 10, y: 20 };


// Implementation of methods associated with the struct

impl Point {

 // A method to calculate the distance from the origin

 fn distance_from_origin(&self) -> f64 {

  ((self.x.pow(2) + self.y.pow(2)) as f64).sqrt()

 }

}


// Using the method on an instance of the struct

let distance = p.distance_from_origin();

println!("Distance from origin: {}", distance);
```

The above sample program outlines the creation of a **Point** struct with two integer fields, **x** and **y**. Methods can be defined using **impl** blocks that allow instances of the struct to perform specific operations such as calculating a point's distance from the origin.

Advantages

- Structs allow encapsulation of data, meaning that the data and the operations on that data are bound together. This encapsulation simplifies code management and enhances data integrity.

- By defining a struct, you create a blueprint that can be used to instantiate multiple objects, facilitating code reuse and reducing redundancy.

- Rust's type system ensures that structs are used consistently throughout the program, catching type errors at compile time and preventing common bugs associated with dynamic typing.

- Compared to more dynamic data structures (like hash maps), structs are generally more memory efficient and faster, as they allow static dispatch and have predictable memory layouts.

- Structs are widely used in both simple and complex programming scenarios, such as:

  - Representing entities like a **User** or a **Product** in a business application.

  - Storing configurations as in the case of settings for a software application.

  - Modeling objects in a game, such as players, monsters, or terrains.

Types of Structs

There are several different types of structs in Rust. We shall explore these types along with examples, expanding on the basic **Point** struct used previously as below:

Tuple Structs

Tuple structs are essentially named tuples. They are useful when you want to give a whole tuple a name for clarity but don't need to name each field individually.

```
struct Color(i32, i32, i32);



let white = Color(255, 255, 255);

println!("White RGB is ({}, {}, {})", white.0, white.1,
white.2);
```

In the above code snippet, **Color** is a tuple struct with three **i32** fields representing RGB values. Tuple structs are accessed via their indices, similar to tuples.

Unit-Like Structs

Unit-like structs do not have any fields and are useful in situations where you need to implement a trait but don't need to store any data.

```
struct Empty;


impl Empty {

  fn new() -> Self {

  Empty

  }

}



let empty = Empty::new();
```

In the above, **Empty** is a unit-like struct that serves as a placeholder or marker and can have methods associated with it.

Classic C-Style Structs

These are the most common structs and are similar to structs in C or C++. They allow you to name and store various pieces of data together.

```
struct Point {

  x: i32,

  y: i32,

}



impl Point {
```

```rust
fn distance_from_origin(&self) -> f64 {

    ((self.x.pow(2) + self.y.pow(2)) as f64).sqrt()

    }

}


let point = Point { x: 10, y: 20 };

println!("Distance from origin: {}",
point.distance_from_origin());
```

This **Point** struct is a typical example of a classic C-style struct, where **x** and **y** are named fields of the struct, and methods can be implemented to perform operations related to the data stored in the struct.

Each type of struct has its place in Rust programming:

- Tuple structs are used when you need a simple way to bundle together some values without the overhead of naming each field.

- Unit-like structs are often used in generic programming and meta-programming when behavior is more important than data.

- Classic structs are the most frequently used, as they combine data storage with behaviors, making code easier to manage and more object-oriented.

Writing Program Using Struct

Structuring data effectively is key to building well-organized software, and the following **Student** struct is a perfect example of how real-world entities can be modeled within a program. In the below sample program, the **Student** struct encapsulates all the necessary attributes of a student, making it easier to manage and utilize student data across the application.

```rust
// Definition of the Student struct

struct Student {

    id: i32,
```

```rust
    name: String,

    major: String,

    year: i32,

}


// Implementing methods for the Student struct

impl Student {

    // Constructor to create a new Student

    fn new(id: i32, name: &str, major: &str, year: i32) -> Self {

    Self {

    id,

    name: name.to_string(),

    major: major.to_string(),

    year,

    }

    }


    // Method to calculate GPA based on a slice of integer grades

    fn calculate_gpa(&self, grades: &[i32]) -> f64 {

    let sum: i32 = grades.iter().sum();
```

```rust
    let num_grades = grades.len() as f64;

    sum as f64 / num_grades

    }


    // Method to display student information

    fn display(&self) {

    println!("Student ID: {}, Name: {}, Major: {}, Year: {}", self.id, self.name, self.major, self.year);

    }

}


fn main() {

    // Creating instances of Student

    let s1 = Student::new(1, "Alice", "Computer Science", 3);

    let s2 = Student::new(2, "Bob", "Physics", 4);

    let s3 = Student::new(3, "Charlie", "Chemistry", 2);


    // Example of calculating GPA

    let s1_gpa = s1.calculate_gpa(&[90, 95, 80]);

    println!("GPA of {}: {}", s1.name, s1_gpa);
```

```
// Displaying student information

s1.display();

s2.display();

s3.display();

}
```

In the above code snippet,

- Struct Initialization: The **new** method acts as a constructor, simplifying the instantiation of **Student** objects.

- Method **calculate_gpa**: This method calculates the GPA based on a list of grades, demonstrating how to add behavior that operates on the data within a struct.

- Method **display**: A utility method to print out student details, showcasing how methods can provide additional functionality to a struct.

Aside from improving the readability and overall robustness of your Rust applications, this method of using structs effectively organizes data. A solid foundation for modeling complex entities and managing their behavior predictably is provided by structures equipped with methods.

Using Custom Structs

Custom structs allow you to define your own data types tailored to the specific needs of your application, giving you the flexibility to encapsulate related data and behaviors in an organized manner.

Following is a quick example of how you can utilize custom structs effectively:.

```
// Definition of the custom struct Person

struct Person {

 name: String,

 age: u8,

}
```

```rust
// Implementing methods for the Person struct

impl Person {

 // Constructor method to create a new Person instance

 fn new(name: &str, age: u8) -> Self {

 Self {

 name: name.to_string(),

 age,

 }

 }


 // Method to display a greeting from the person

 fn say_hello(&self) {

 println!("Hello, my name is {} and I am {} years old.",
self.name, self.age);

 }

}


fn main() {

 // Creating instances of the Person struct using the new
constructor

 let p1 = Person::new("Alice", 30);
```

```
let p2 = Person::new("Bob", 40);



// Calling the method on the Person instances

p1.say_hello();

p2.say_hello();

}
```

Writing Custom Struct Program

Building on the previous introduction to custom structs in Rust, we now delve deeper into a practical example, illustrating how to define and use a custom type to manage geometrical data effectively.

Sample Program: Custom Struct for Rectangle

This below example includes both a method to calculate the area of the rectangle and an associated function for creating new instances.

```
// Definition of the Rectangle struct

struct Rectangle {

 width: u32,

 height: u32,

}



// Implementation of methods and associated functions for Rectangle

impl Rectangle {
```

```rust
// Constructor for creating a new Rectangle

fn new(width: u32, height: u32) -> Self {

Rectangle { width, height }

}


// Method to calculate the area of the Rectangle

fn area(&self) -> u32 {

self.width * self.height

}

}


fn main() {

// Creating instances of Rectangle using the new
associated function

let r1 = Rectangle::new(10, 20);

let r2 = Rectangle::new(5, 15);


// Accessing fields and calculating area

println!("The width of r1 is {}, and the height is {}",
r1.width, r1.height);

println!("The area of r1 is {}", r1.area());

println!("The area of r2 is {}", r2.area());
```

```
}
```

Key Features and Advantages

- The **Rectangle** struct encapsulates the properties of a rectangle, namely its width and height. This organization makes the data easy to manage and operations on the data straightforward to perform.

- By implementing the **area** method, the struct not only holds data but also behavior, making the **Rectangle** struct more versatile and self-contained.

- The **new** function (an associated function) simplifies creating new instances of **Rectangle**, ensuring that all required properties are set at creation time, which enhances the robustness and integrity of the data.

The **Rectangle** struct has several potential real-world uses, including representing screen regions, managing window dimensions, and detecting collisions between graphical objects. It is commonly found in graphics rendering engines and window management systems.

Writing a Nested Structs

Nested structs provide a way to structure related data more complexly and intuitively, making your code cleaner and more organized. Given below is how you can implement nested structs effectively.

Example of Nested Structs in Rust

Following is an example that demonstrates how to define and use nested structs along with method implementations:

```
// Definition of the InnerStruct

struct InnerStruct {

  field3: i32,

  field4: i32,

}
```

```rust
// Methods for InnerStruct
impl InnerStruct {
 fn new(field3: i32, field4: i32) -> Self {
 Self { field3, field4 }
 }


 fn sum(&self) -> i32 {
 self.field3 + self.field4
 }
}


// Definition of the OuterStruct which includes
InnerStruct as a field
struct OuterStruct {
 field1: i32,
 field2: i32,
 nested: InnerStruct,
}


// Methods for OuterStruct
impl OuterStruct {
```

```rust
    fn new(field1: i32, field2: i32, nested: InnerStruct) ->
Self {

    Self { field1, field2, nested }

    }


    fn details(&self) {

    println!("field1: {}, field2: {}", self.field1,
self.field2);

    println!("Nested field3: {}, field4: {}",
self.nested.field3, self.nested.field4);

    }

}


fn main() {

    let inner = InnerStruct::new(10, 20);

    let outer = OuterStruct::new(1, 2, inner);


    outer.details();

    println!("The sum of nested fields: {}",
outer.nested.sum());

}
```

In the above code snippet,

- The **InnerStruct** is defined with two integer fields. It includes a constructor for easy initialization and a method to calculate the sum of its fields.

- The **OuterStruct** includes **InnerStruct** as one of its fields, demonstrating the nesting. It also has its own fields and a method to print details of the struct, including those of the nested **InnerStruct**.

- The **main** function demonstrates creating instances of **InnerStruct** and **OuterStruct**. It shows how to access methods of the nested struct and how to interact with the fields directly.

Benefits

- Nested structs allow for better organization of complex data. They make it clear how different pieces of data are related and can help manage them more efficiently.

- By nesting structs, you can encapsulate specific behaviors and data closely related to those behaviors within an appropriate context.

- Code with nested structs is generally easier to maintain because it mimics real-world data structures more closely, making the codebase easier to understand and modify.

Nested structs are particularly useful in scenarios where you have layered or hierarchical data relationships, such as graphical user interfaces, complex business logic, or data models that mirror real-world objects.

Struct Inheritance

Direct struct inheritance, in which one struct can inherit the attributes and methods of another, is not supported in Rust. This is in contrast to other programming languages. Rust, on the other hand, permits comparable functionality via its composition and traits, offering flexibility while still maintaining its safety and performance principles.

Sample Program: Composition for Struct Inheritance

Following is an example of using composition to simulate inheritance in Rust:

```
struct BaseStruct {

  field1: i32,

  field2: i32,

}
```

```rust
impl BaseStruct {
  fn sum(&self) -> i32 {
  self.field1 + self.field2
  }
}


struct DerivedStruct {
  base: BaseStruct,
  field3: i32,
}


fn main() {
  let base = BaseStruct { field1: 1, field2: 2 };
  let derived = DerivedStruct { base, field3: 3 };

  println!("The value of field1 is {}",
derived.base.field1);
  println!("The value of field2 is {}",
derived.base.field2);
  println!("The sum of base fields is {}",
derived.base.sum());
```

```
}
```

In the above sample program, **DerivedStruct** contains an instance of **BaseStruct**, allowing it to utilize **BaseStruct**'s fields and methods. This composition mimics inheritance by giving **DerivedStruct** access to the functionalities of **BaseStruct**.

Using Traits for Inheritance-like Behavior

Another method to achieve similar behavior is through the use of traits, which can be seen as a way to define shared behavior across structs.

```
trait BaseTrait {

  fn sum(&self) -> i32;

}



struct BaseStruct {

  field1: i32,

  field2: i32,

}



impl BaseTrait for BaseStruct {

  fn sum(&self) -> i32 {

  self.field1 + self.field2

  }

}
```

```rust
struct DerivedStruct<'a> {

 base: &'a dyn BaseTrait,

 field3: i32,

}


fn main() {

 let base = BaseStruct { field1: 10, field2: 20 };

 let derived = DerivedStruct { base: &base, field3: 5 };


 println!("The sum from BaseTrait is {}",
derived.base.sum());

 println!("Additional field in derived struct: {}",
derived.field3);

}
```

The above sample program illustrates how **DerivedStruct** holds a reference to something that implements the **BaseTrait** trait, allowing it to use methods defined by **BaseTrait**. This approach is highly flexible and powerful, especially for polymorphic behavior.

Using either composition or trait objects demonstrates that Rust can handle complicated data structures and behaviors. Rust ensures that data structures have distinct boundaries and relationships by utilizing composition. The combination of traits with generic programming allows for polymorphic code and allows for the sharing of behaviors.

Do's and Don'ts

Following are some practical do's and don'ts for using structs in Rust, along with illustrated examples to practically experience the do's and don'ts.

Do's of Using Structs

Use Structs for Fixed Data Structures

Structs should be used to represent data that has a fixed number of fields with well-defined types.

For example:

```
struct Book {

 title: String,

 author: String,

 pages: u32,

}
```

Use Named Fields for Clarity

Always use named fields in your structs to clarify the purpose of each field.

For example:

```
struct Point {

 x: f64,

 y: f64,

}
```

Add Behavior with Methods

Use methods to add functionality related to the data the structs hold.

For example:

```
impl Point {

 fn distance_to_origin(&self) -> f64 {

 (self.x.powi(2) + self.y.powi(2)).sqrt()
```

```
  }

}
```

Use Associated Functions for Construction

Associated functions are used for operations that do not require an instance of the struct, typically used for construction.

For example:

```
impl Point {

  fn new(x: f64, y: f64) -> Point {

  Point { x, y }

  }

}
```

Implement Impl Blocks

Use **impl** blocks to define both methods and associated functions.

This organizes functionalities related to the struct neatly.

Consider Composition for Reuse

Use nested structs or composition to reuse fields or methods across multiple structs.

For example:

```
struct Circle {

  center: Point,

  radius: f64,

}
```

Use Trait Objects for Flexibility

Consider using trait objects to allow for structs that can handle multiple types that implement a particular trait.

For example:

```
trait Shape {

  fn area(&self) -> f64;

}


struct ShapeBox {

  shape: Box<dyn Shape>,

}
```

Don'ts of Using Structs

Avoid Structs for Variable Data Structures

Do not use structs for data that can vary in number of fields or field types. Use enums with variants instead.

Example of What Not to Do:

```
// Incorrect usage for variable data types

struct UserData {

  data: Vec<String>, // Unclear and unspecific structure

}
```

Avoid Anonymous Fields

Do not use anonymous fields as they can obscure the purpose of each field.

Example of What Not to Do:

```
struct Pair(i32, i32); // Avoid if clarity is essential
```

Avoid Unnecessary Mutation

Do not define methods that mutate the struct unless necessary. Use **&self** for non-mutating methods.

 For example:

```
impl Book {

  fn add_page(&mut self) {

  self.pages += 1;

  }

}
```

Manage Lifetime of References Carefully

Avoid returning references to the struct's fields unless you are certain about the lifetimes involved.

Example of What Not to Do:

```
impl Book {

  fn title(&self) -> &String {

  &self.title // Be cautious with lifetimes

  }

}
```

If you follow these dos and don'ts, you will be able to make effective use of Rust's struct functionality, which will allow you to construct applications that are both secure and effective.

Summary

As a core data structuring tool in Rust, struct is thoroughly explored in this chapter to help developers create code that is well-organized, efficient, and safe. Each struct has its own set of fields with clearly defined types; these fields are used to represent data that has a fixed structure. Each of the three main categories of structs covered in this chapter—traditional, tuple, and unit structs—serves a unique function in data management.

Traditional structs, as described in the chapter, are similar to classes in other languages but do not have inheritance capabilities built in. In order to create a codebase that is both modular and easy to maintain, Rust promotes the usage of structs within structs and places an emphasis on composition rather than inheritance. As an example of hierarchical data composition, developers can build complex structs by embedding other structs within them.

This chapter spends a lot of time explaining how to put these ideas into practice using custom structs, which are great for enclosing data and related functions. To improve the struct's usability and functionality, we dove into writing custom structs with methods and associated functions, demonstrating how to add behaviors like methods to calculate values or perform actions.

Sharing information on the "dos and don'ts" also gives important pointers for making good use of structs. Named fields improve readability, methods control behavior, and composition is better than inheritance for adding new features, among other best practices covered. It also warns about typical mistakes like returning references that might outlive the struct or using structs for variable data structures.

This chapter taught developers how to make the most of structs, a powerful feature for creating robust applications, by providing examples and conceptual explanation.

CHAPTER 5: ENUMS AND PATTERN MATCHING

Introduction

In this chapter, we will explore the robust and flexible features of Rust's enums and pattern matching. Enums are defined in this chapter as a way to describe a type by listing all of its possible variants. For types that can take on a fixed set of values, enums are a lifesaver, making your code more expressive and secure.

This chapter will teach you the ins and outs of pattern matching, a technique for comparing a value to a set of patterns and then running code depending on which pattern is a match. Concise and powerful control flow structures are made possible by this feature's deep integration with enums.

The chapter will begin with an overview of enums and then proceed to show you how to define and use them to represent concepts in your code that can vary across a fixed set of possibilities. It will walk you through writing programs that incorporate enums from scratch, starting with the basics.

Subsequently, we will go on to more advanced topics regarding match expressions. Beyond basic matching, you'll learn advanced pattern matching techniques like destructuring, guard matching, and more.

Decisions based on enum-represented states are also covered in the chapter, along with pattern matching in control flow. In this section, we will see how pattern matching and enums work together to make code that is more stable and less prone to errors.

The chapter will end with some recommendations for improving your pattern matching in Rust as well as some common pitfalls to avoid. By doing so, you can be sure that you have a firm grasp on these features and can apply them idiomatically and effectively in your Rust code.

Enum Basics

One effective method of defining a type that can have multiple defined values, or variants, is using an enum. They shine when you need to model ideas in your code with a limited number of states or options. We shall take a closer look at enums:

Definition

Enums are declared using the **enum** keyword, followed by the name of the enum and a set of variants enclosed in curly braces. Given below is an example of the **Suit** enum, which represents the four suits in a deck of cards:

```
enum Suit {

  Spades,
```

```
  Hearts,

  Diamonds,

  Clubs,

}



// Creating an instance of the Suit enum

let my_suit = Suit::Spades;
```

In the above code snippet, **Suit** has four variants: **Spades**, **Hearts**, **Diamonds**, and **Clubs**. You can create an instance of **Suit** by specifying one of these variants. Enums are a way to group related values with semantics that describe your data more accurately than simple types like integers or strings.

Enum with Associated Data

Enums can also carry associated data with each variant, which can be of any type. This is useful for creating complex data structures where each variant might need to hold different types of data.

Given below is an example of an enum that represents playing cards, where each card has a suit associated with it:

```
enum Card {

  Ace(Suit),

  King(Suit),

  Queen(Suit),

  Jack(Suit),

  Number(u8, Suit),

}
```

```
// Creating an instance of the Card enum with associated
data

let my_card = Card::Ace(Suit::Spades);

let another_card = Card::Number(7, Suit::Hearts);
```

In this **Card** enum, each variant can carry a **Suit** type except for **Number**, which carries both a numeric value and a suit. This model allows for flexibility and clarity in how data is structured and managed within your program.

Enum Methods

You can also define methods on enums using **impl** blocks, which can perform operations based on the enum's current state:

```
impl Card {

 fn display(&self) -> String {

 match self {

  Card::Ace(suit) => format!("Ace of {:?}", suit),

  Card::King(suit) => format!("King of {:?}", suit),

  Card::Queen(suit) => format!("Queen of {:?}", suit),

  Card::Jack(suit) => format!("Jack of {:?}", suit),

  Card::Number(number, suit) => format!("{} of {:?}",
number, suit),

  }

 }

}
```

```
// Using the display method

let card_description = my_card.display();

println!("{}", card_description);
```

This method, **display**, returns a formatted string describing the card. The **match** expression is used to pattern match on **self**, allowing different behavior depending on which variant of **Card** is being handled.

Pattern Matching

Overview

A strong feature of Rust, pattern matching enables developers to handle variants of enums concisely and robustly. Compared to the conventional switch-case statements used in other languages, it allows for more expressive and error-resistant control flow by executing different branches of code depending on the state of an enum.

Following is a sample program of using pattern matching with enums in Rust:

```
// Define an enum for Suit

enum Suit {

  Spades,

  Hearts,

  Diamonds,

  Clubs,

}
```

```rust
// Example of using pattern matching to handle different
suits

fn print_suit(suit: Suit) {

 match suit {

 Suit::Spades => println!("The suit is spades"),

 Suit::Hearts => println!("The suit is hearts"),

 Suit::Diamonds => println!("The suit is diamonds"),

 Suit::Clubs => println!("The suit is clubs"),

 }

}


// Define an enum for Card with associated data

enum Card {

 Ace(Suit),

 King(Suit),

 Queen(Suit),

 Jack(Suit),

 Number(u8, Suit),

}


// Using pattern matching to destructure and handle
different cards
```

```
fn print_card(card: Card) {

 match card {

 Card::Ace(suit) => println!("The card is an Ace of
{:?}", suit),

 Card::King(suit) => println!("The card is a King of
{:?}", suit),

 Card::Queen(suit) => println!("The card is a Queen of
{:?}", suit),

 Card::Jack(suit) => println!("The card is a Jack of
{:?}", suit),

 Card::Number(number, suit) => println!("The card is a {}
of {:?}", number, suit),

 }

}


// Creating instances of Suit and Card

let my_suit = Suit::Spades;

let my_card = Card::Ace(Suit::Spades);


// Calling the functions

print_suit(my_suit);

print_card(my_card);
```

In practical applications, pattern matching is often used to decode messages, handle various states of application logic, and process complex data structures without resorting to verbose and error-prone if-else chains.

Key Features

- Pattern matching provides a methodical way to execute different branches of code based on the enum variant. This is particularly useful for enums with associated data, as it allows not only for matching against different variants but also for destructuring these variants to access their internal data.

- Using **match** expressions makes the code more readable and less prone to errors. Rust's compiler ensures that all possible cases are handled or explicitly ignored (using _), which prevents bugs related to unhandled cases.

- Pattern matching is not limited to enums. It can be used with other Rust types, such as tuples and structs, to extract values directly through pattern matching.

Advantages of Enum and Pattern Matching

You can handle structured data more securely, more clearly, and more efficiently with the help of enums and pattern matching. We shall get into these advantages with precise examples:

Type Safety

Enums enforce type safety by allowing you to define a type with a fixed set of variants. This prevents the kind of errors that arise from using arbitrary integers or strings to represent state, which can lead to invalid states or values.

```rust
enum TrafficLight {

  Red,

  Yellow,

  Green,

}


fn react_to_light(light: TrafficLight) {

  match light {
```

```
    TrafficLight::Red => println!("Stop"),

    TrafficLight::Yellow => println!("Caution"),

    TrafficLight::Green => println!("Go"),

    }

}
```

In the above code snippet, **TrafficLight** ensures that only valid states are representable, reducing errors associated with invalid states.

Readability

Enums paired with pattern matching can greatly increase the readability of your code by making the control flow explicit and declarative.

```
enum HttpStatus {

    Ok,

    NotFound,

    InternalServerError,

}


fn handle_request(status: HttpStatus) {

    match status {

    HttpStatus::Ok => println!("Request succeeded"),

    HttpStatus::NotFound => println!("Resource not found"),

    HttpStatus::InternalServerError => println!("An internal
server error occurred"),
```

```
  }

}
```

This approach makes it clear what each branch of logic does for each **HttpStatus** variant, improving maintainability and readability, especially for those unfamiliar with the codebase.

Conciseness

Using enums and pattern matching can lead to more concise code by reducing the need for verbose if-else chains.

```
enum AgeCategory {

 Minor,

 Adult,

 Senior,

}


struct Person {

 age: u8,

}


fn classify_person(person: Person) -> AgeCategory {

 match person.age {

 age if age < 18 => AgeCategory::Minor,

 age if age < 65 => AgeCategory::Adult,

 _ => AgeCategory::Senior,
```

```
    }

}
```

This refactoring with enums and **match** statements streamlines the function, making it easier to modify and extend.

Overall, enums and pattern matching provide clear benefits over traditional coding practices by ensuring type safety, improving code readability and maintainability, and often enhancing performance.

'match' Expression

Rust's pattern matching is a highly expressive feature that allows for detailed control over program flow based on the shape and value of data. We shall explore deep into some of the advanced aspects of pattern matching:

Matching Multiple Patterns

Rust allows you to match multiple patterns using the **|** operator. This can simplify cases where multiple patterns execute the same block of code.

```
let x = 3;


match x {

 1 | 2 | 3 => println!("x is 1, 2, or 3"),

 _ => println!("x is something else"),

}
```

If **x** is 1, 2, or 3, the same line of code is executed, reducing redundancy.

Matching Ranges

You can match a range of values using the **..=** syntax, which is handy for grouping multiple consecutive values together.

```
let x = 5;


match x {

  1..=5 => println!("x is between 1 and 5"),

  _ => println!("x is something else"),

}
```

This matches any value from 1 to 5, inclusive.

Destructuring for Pattern Matching

Rust allows you to destructure tuples, arrays, structs, and enums directly in a match statement, making it straightforward to access their components.

```
struct Point {

  x: i32,

  y: i32,

}


let p = Point { x: 3, y: 4 };


match p {

  Point { x, y } => println!("Point coordinates are x: {},
y: {}", x, y),

}
```

This destructures **Point** and binds **x** and **y** to values from the struct.

Guards in Match Arms

Guards allow for additional conditions to be specified within a match arm, using the **if** keyword after the pattern.

```
let x = 3;



match x {

  y if y % 2 == 0 => println!("x is even"),

  y if y % 2 == 1 => println!("x is odd"),

  _ => println!("x is something else"),

}
```

The above code snippet uses guards to check whether a number is even or odd.

Matching on References

Matching on references involves dereferencing with **&**, and sometimes using patterns to directly match on the dereferenced values.

```
let x = 3;

match &x {

  &y if y > 3 => println!("x is greater than 3"),

  &y if y < 3 => println!("x is less than 3"),

  _ => println!("x is equal to 3"),

}
```

The Rust programming language does not have an is operator to check types directly in match arms. Rust uses strict static typing, and the type of a variable must be known at compile time. If you need type-based logic, consider using traits and trait objects.

Using Control Flow

Using control flow in conjunction with enums and pattern matching allows for clear and efficient handling of different cases based on enum variants. This approach is much more structured compared to traditional if-else chains, particularly when dealing with complex data types.

Using "if let" for Simple Matching

The **if let** syntax is ideal for cases where you only need to match one pattern and ignore the others, making your code cleaner and more readable:

```
enum HttpStatus {

 Ok,

 NotFound,

 InternalServerError,

 Unauthorized,

}


fn handle_request(status: HttpStatus) {

 if let HttpStatus::Ok = status {

 println!("Request succeeded");

 } else if let HttpStatus::NotFound = status {

 println!("Resource not found");

 } else if let HttpStatus::InternalServerError = status {

 println!("An internal server error occurred");

 } else {

 println!("Unhandled status");
```

```
    }

}
```

In this code, **if let** is used to selectively execute code blocks based on the enum variant of **status**. This approach is succinct for a few conditions but might not be the best choice for more extensive pattern matching.

Using match for Comprehensive Pattern Matching

For a more exhaustive handling of enums, the **match** statement is generally more appropriate because it ensures that all possible cases are considered, and it's cleaner when you have multiple patterns to handle:

```
fn handle_request(status: HttpStatus) {

  match status {

   HttpStatus::Ok => println!("Request succeeded"),

   HttpStatus::NotFound => println!("Resource not found"),

   HttpStatus::InternalServerError => println!("An internal
server error occurred"),

   HttpStatus::Unauthorized => println!("Unauthorized
access"),

  }

}
```

In the above, **match** comprehensively covers all potential enum variants, which enhances both safety and clarity by forcing you to handle each case explicitly.

Control Flow with Enums having Associated Data

For enums that include associated data, you can also use **if let** or **match** to destructure and access the data:

```rust
enum Card {

 Ace(Suit),

 Number(u8, Suit),

 Face(String, Suit),

}


fn handle_card(card: Card) {

 match card {

 Card::Ace(suit) => println!("The card is an Ace of
{:?}", suit),

 Card::Number(value, suit) => println!("The card is a {}
of {:?}", value, suit),

 Card::Face(face, suit) => println!("The card is a {} of
{:?}", face, suit),

 }

}
```

The above code snippet uses **match** to not only handle each variant of the **Card** enum but also to extract and use the associated data (such as the card value and suit) directly within each branch. This pattern is very powerful and allows for clear, concise, and type-safe handling of complex data structures.

Do's and Don'ts

Do's of Enum and Pattern Matching

Use Enums for Defined States

Enums are perfect for representing a specific set of options or states within your application. This can increase the readability and robustness of your code.

For example:

```
enum TrafficLight {

  Red,

  Yellow,

  Green,

}
```

Leverage Pattern Matching for Clarity

Use pattern matching to execute different branches of code based on an enum's current state. This approach is cleaner than using multiple if-else conditions.

For example:

```
let light = TrafficLight::Red;

match light {

  TrafficLight::Red => println!("Stop"),

  TrafficLight::Yellow => println!("Caution"),

  TrafficLight::Green => println!("Go"),

}
```

Use a Catch-All Pattern

Always include a _ pattern in your match statements to handle unexpected or future values gracefully.

For example:

```
let number = 5;
```

```
match number {

 1 => println!("One"),

 2 => println!("Two"),

 _ => println!("Other"),

}
```

Use *if let for Single Matches*

When only one pattern is of interest, **if let** is a concise alternative to **match** that avoids boilerplate.

For example:

```
let some_option = Some(7);

if let Some(x) = some_option {

 println!("Found {}", x);

}
```

Don'ts of Enum and Pattern Matching

Don't Omit the Catch-All Pattern

Failing to include a catch-all pattern in match expressions could lead to runtime panics if none of the specified patterns are matched.

Example to avoid:

```
let num = 10;

match num {

 1 => println!("One"),

 2 => println!("Two"),
```

```
  // This will panic if num is not 1 or 2

}
```

Avoid Side Effects in Match Arms

Try to avoid using match expressions solely to perform actions that don't return a value. Structuring your code this way can lead to confusion and bugs.

Example to avoid:

```
match command {

  Command::Start => start_service(),

  Command::Stop => stop_service(),

  _ => log_error(),

}

// Better to use if or while for repeated side effects
```

Adhering to these practices will help you harness the full potential of enums and pattern matching in Rust, leading to clearer, more effective, and safer code.

Summary

Enums and Pattern Matching are the main topics of this chapter. To improve type safety, enums let developers define types with a fixed set of variants rather than the variable-based primitive type constants that can lead to invalid states. Establishing this foundation is crucial for developing code structures that are easy to understand and maintain, and for conveying the capabilities and uses of different data states in applications.

When used in conjunction with enums, pattern matching provides a mechanism to run code depending on an enum's state. By utilizing match statements, developers can precisely handle enum variants, taking into consideration all potential scenarios; this not only prevents runtime errors but also simplifies debugging. You can use pattern matching to destructur structs and tuples as well as enums, which allows you to handle complex data structures in a concise and flexible way.

For less complex cases requiring only one pattern match, the chapter delves further into the intricacies of using if let to avoid the verbosity of full match expressions. It demonstrated how crucial it is to incorporate a catch-all pattern into match statements at all times in order to gracefully handle unexpected cases and avoid runtime panics.

The use of pattern guards to fine-tune match conditions and the advantages of matching on ranges and multiple patterns at once were among the more complex topics covered. There is some practical advice given, like only using pattern matching in parts of code that are really important for performance and not for side effects that could make the code less clear and more prone to errors.

In sum, this chapter taught developers how to make good use of enums and pattern matching, which in turn makes their software more reliable and easier to maintain.

CHAPTER 6: EXPLORING OWNERSHIP AND BORROWING

Introduction

To comprehend how Rust securely and effectively handles memory without a garbage collector, it is essential to familiarize oneself with the fundamental ideas of ownership and borrowing in Rust, which are covered in depth in this chapter. The ownership rules and behaviors that govern the management of memory and resources in Rust programs are explained in this chapter. Important aspects of ownership, such as its transferability and its role in facilitating appropriate resource cleanup, will be covered in this chapter.

Borrowing, another critical feature that permits access to data without assuming ownership of it, will also be learned. That way, various sections of your program can access the same data without jeopardizing memory safety. We will delve deeply into the rules of borrowing, including mutable and immutable references, and how they affect the behavior of programs.

Also covered in this chapter are the distinctions between reference-dependent variables and stack-allocated variables. By seeing how the ownership and borrowing mechanics in Rust manifest in real-world coding scenarios, you'll gain a better grasp of when and how to apply these principles. You will also learn about the practical applications of ownership and borrowing in Rust's standard library and other libraries to guarantee safe memory management and concurrency.

With the knowledge you gain from this chapter, you will be able to write efficient and reliable Rust applications by utilizing ownership and borrowing to achieve memory safety without compromising performance.

Ownership Basics

What is Ownership?

Ownership is a set of rules enforced by Rust's compiler to manage memory and other resources automatically. It eliminates common bugs such as null pointer dereferencing, memory leaks, and data races in concurrent contexts.

The ownership system is built around three main rules:

- Each value has a variable called its owner.

- There can be only one owner at a time.

- When the owner goes out of scope, the value will be dropped (i.e., memory is freed).

Features of Ownership

Memory Safety without Garbage Collection

Unlike languages that use garbage collection, Rust uses ownership to ensure memory safety. This means that memory is automatically cleaned up when an object's owner variable goes out of scope, preventing memory leaks.

Prevention of Data Races

Ownership plays a crucial role in concurrent programming. By ensuring that certain data is owned by only one variable at a time, Rust prevents data races, which occur when two or more threads access the same memory concurrently and at least one of them is writing.

Efficient Memory Use

Because memory is automatically returned to the system when it is no longer needed (i.e., when the owner variable goes out of scope), Rust programs often use memory more efficiently and run faster.

Ownership Transfer

Ownership can be transferred through assignment or function calls. This is known as "moving." When the ownership of a resource is transferred from one variable to another, the original variable can no longer be used to access the resource. This prevents "double free" errors, where two variables attempt to free the same resource.

```
let s1 = String::from("hello");

let s2 = s1; // Ownership of the string is moved to s2

// println!("{s1}"); This line would cause a compile-time
error because s1 no longer owns the string
```

Copy Trait

Not all types are subject to ownership rules in the same way. Types that implement the **Copy** trait, like integers and other simple scalar values, do not move in the same way as types that do not implement **Copy**. Instead, they are copied when assigned to another variable or passed to functions.

```
let x = 5;

let y = x; // x can still be used because integers are
`Copy`
```

The strict enforcement by the Rust compiler ensures that any violations of ownership rules are caught before runtime, making Rust programs exceptionally reliable and secure.

Borrowing Overview

A basic idea that lets you access data without actually owning it is borrowing. This is a crucial component of Rust's method for concurrency and memory safety that doesn't involve a garbage collector. Both immutable and mutable borrowing have their own set of rules that ensure the program doesn't have data races or any other typical bugs.

We shall take a closer look at Rust's borrowing and references as below:

Immutable Borrowing

Immutable borrowing allows you to create a reference to a value without taking ownership. This type of borrowing allows multiple parts of your code to read the data without modification, ensuring that the data remains unchanged:

```
let s = String::from("hello");

let ref1 = &s;

let ref2 = &s;



println!("{}, world!", ref1);
```

In the above code snippet, **s** is borrowed immutably by **ref1** and **ref2**. You can have any number of immutable references to a variable, as long as there are no mutable references to the same variable at the same time.

Mutable Borrowing

Mutable borrowing allows you to create a single mutable reference to a value. This reference can be used to modify the data:

```
let mut s = String::from("hello");

let ref1 = &mut s;
```

```
ref1.push_str(", world!");

println!("{}", ref1);
```

Mutable borrowing is exclusive; while a mutable borrow exists, no other references (either mutable or immutable) can be created. This exclusivity prevents data races, where two pointers access the same data concurrently and at least one of them modifies it.

Rules of Borrowing

Rust's borrowing rules are enforced at compile time by the borrow checker, and they include:

1. You can have either any number of immutable references (&T) or exactly one mutable reference (&mut T).

2. A reference must not outlive the data it points to.

3. You cannot have a reference to data that has been deallocated.

Lifetimes

A key part of borrowing is the concept of 'lifetimes', which are implicit or explicit annotations that tell the Rust compiler about how long references should be valid. The compiler uses lifetimes to ensure references do not outlive the data they refer to, thus preventing dangling pointers.

```
fn main() {

  let r; // ------+-- 'a

  // |

  { // |

  let x = 5; // -+-- 'b

  r = &x; // | |

  } // -+ |

  // |

  println!("r: {}", r); // |
```

```
}  //  ------+
```

In the above code snippet, the code will fail to compile because **r** tries to reference **x** after **x** has been deallocated. The use of borrowing is pervasive in Rust programming, ranging from controlling access patterns in complex data structures like graphs and trees to more basic data access. More expressive code, better memory management, and safe concurrency patterns are all made possible by it.

Stack-allocated Variables and References

Stack-Allocated Variables

Variables are, by default, stack-allocated unless explicitly managed to be stored on the heap. Stack-allocated variables are known for their high performance due to the efficiency of memory allocation and deallocation, which happens at compile time and does not require complex management like heap allocation does.

The stack is a region of memory that stores values in a last-in, first-out manner. This means that variables created on the stack can be pushed onto the stack when they come into scope and popped off the stack when they go out of scope. This straightforward allocation and deallocation mechanism makes stack operations very fast.

Characteristics of Stack-Allocated Variables

- Memory access on the stack is faster than on the heap because the stack is tightly managed by the system and typically resides in high-speed memory.

- Memory for stack-allocated variables is automatically managed, which means there is no need to explicitly allocate or free memory.

- The size of stack-allocated variables must be known at compile time and cannot grow dynamically; this is why types that require dynamic sizing, like vectors or strings, are allocated on the heap.

- Stack-allocated variables are bound to the scope in which they are declared. When the scope ends, the variables are deallocated.

References

References are used to borrow the value they point to without taking ownership of it. References are inherently safe because Rust enforces rules at compile time that prevent dangling pointers and data races.

1. Immutable References (**&T**): Allow you to read from but not modify the borrowed data. You can have multiple immutable references to a data point at the same time.

2. Mutable References (**&mut T**): Allow you to modify the borrowed data. You can have only one mutable reference to a particular piece of data in a particular scope. No other mutable references or immutable references to that data are allowed in the same scope.

Sample Program

Consider the previous examples of enums and structs in the context of stack-allocated variables and references:

```
struct Point {

  x: i32,

  y: i32,

}



fn main() {

  let p = Point { x: 10, y: 20 }; // `p` is stack-
allocated

  let p_ref = &p; // `p_ref` is a reference to `p`, stack-
allocated



  println!("Point coordinates: ({}, {})", p_ref.x,
p_ref.y);

  // Accessing `p` via its reference does not involve any
heap allocation

}
```

In the above example:

- **Point** is a simple struct with two integer fields, **x** and **y**.

- **p** is an instance of **Point**, allocated on the stack.

- **p_ref** is a stack-allocated reference to **p**. It allows access to **p** without taking ownership, fitting perfectly into Rust's borrowing rules.

- The data is accessed efficiently without any overhead of heap allocation.

By allocating and referencing the stack, Rust programs are safe and efficient, following the compiler's stringent borrowing rules and taking advantage of the stack for fast access and predictable memory management.

Libraries adopting Ownership and Borrowing

Rust's ownership and borrowing mechanisms are integral to its standard library and many third-party libraries, providing robust safety guarantees and efficient memory management. In the below, we'll explore a few key libraries and components that demonstrate these concepts effectively.

The Rust Standard Library

The Rust standard library itself is a treasure trove of examples that use ownership and borrowing.

Its key areas include:

- Collections: Many of Rust's standard collections like **Vec<T>**, **HashMap<K, V>**, and others use ownership to manage the memory of elements they contain. For instance, when an item is added to a **Vec<T>**, ownership of the item is transferred to the vector, which manages the memory for all its elements.

- Iterators: Iterators extensively use borrowing to allow iteration over collections without taking ownership of the collection. For example, the **.iter()** method on a **Vec<T>** borrows the vector and yields references to its elements, ensuring the vector can be used after iteration.

- Concurrency: Rust's standard library offers several concurrency primitives like **Arc<T>** and **Mutex<T>**, which utilize ownership to manage shared data across multiple threads safely.

Serde

The Serde framework is extensively utilized in the Rust ecosystem for efficient data serialization and deserialization. Without actually owning the full data structure that is being serialized or deserialized, Serde can borrow it to read or write JSON, YAML, and other formats. This method improves performance by reducing the amount of data that needs to be copied.

Rayon

One data parallelism library that simplifies threading a lot is Rayon. It makes use of Rust's ownership and borrowing rules to prevent race conditions caused by data manipulation in parallel operations. Rayon offers a robust and secure model for parallel computation by mandating that data shared across threads be either immutable (and thus securely shareable) or owned by a single thread at a time.

Tokio

Tokio is a Rust asynchronous runtime that can manage many concurrent operations with the help of futures and non-blocking I/O. Within the context of a task, borrowing is used to handle references to resources in a non-blocking manner, while ownership is crucial for managing the lifetimes of asynchronous tasks and their resources in Tokio.

Diesel

Diesel is an ORM (Object-Relational Mapping) library for Rust that provides a safe and expressive interface to work with databases. Diesel utilizes Rust's advanced type system, ownership, and borrowing to ensure that database queries are built safely and efficiently. It uses borrowing to prevent SQL injection attacks and to ensure that references to SQL query elements are valid for the duration of the query construction.

Examples of libraries that put Rust's ownership and borrowing mechanisms into practice include the ones mentioned above; they allow developers to create secure, concurrent, and efficient software.

Summary

In Chapter 6, we explored the complex state of borrowing and ownership in Rust. These fundamental concepts influence the language's memory management and data access mechanisms. To avoid memory leaks and data races, ownership rules ensure every piece of data has one owner. An example of Rust's deterministic memory management that doesn't require a garbage collector is the automatic cleaning up of data owned by variables when they go out of scope.

By enabling immutable or mutable access to data without transferring ownership, borrowing is a useful complement to ownership. Immutable borrowing improves safety by avoiding data races caused by concurrent mutable access by allowing multiple references to data that do not modify it. In contrast, mutable borrowing bolsters Rust's thread safety guarantees by enabling data modification but limiting access to a single mutable reference at a time.

To guarantee secure and efficient management of memory and concurrent operations, these ideas are not just theoretical; they are also integrated into Rust's standard library and a number of third-party libraries. Collections like Vec and smart pointers like Arc, for example, manage ownership transitions and borrowing rules internally, exemplifying these principles. To add to that, libraries such as Rayon and Tokio use these safety guarantees to make asynchronous IO operations efficient and concurrent programming safe.

CHAPTER 7: CARGO, CRATES AND PACKAGES

Introduction

Cargo, crates, and packages are the fundamental building blocks of Rust programming, and this chapter explores them in detail, illuminating their critical functions in efficiently managing code, sharing it, and building upon it. The first step is to get familiar with Cargo, the build system and package manager built into Rust. It simplifies tasks like project compilation, dependency management, and package distribution. As a result, programmers can rest assured that their build environment is consistent and easy to replicate.

Next, we'll go over crates, the building blocks of Rust programs. Crates can be either libraries with reusable functions or binaries with executable code. The purpose and distinction between library crates and binary crates will be defined in this section. After that, we'll go over what packages are, how they involve the Cargo.toml file to define a package and its dependencies, and how a package can contain various crates.

The unique functions and interconnections of Cargo, crates, and packages in Rust's ecosystem can be better understood by comparing and contrasting them. After that, you'll find some real-world examples and instructions for making your very first crate and package from the ground up, complete with a walkthrough of the necessary directory structures, configuration files, and compilation steps.

The rest of the chapter will show you how to use Cargo to manage and update dependencies effectively, and it will also walk you through accessing and modifying external packages. Also covered will be the function of Rust's path syntax and module system in arranging and retrieving code from packages and crates, with an emphasis on how these aspects aid in safe and effective code administration.

This chapter will teach you all you need to know about Rust's project management and dependency resolution features, so you can use them to your advantage when creating complex software systems.

Understanding Cargo

Rust's project management system is strengthened by Cargo, which simplifies the process of constructing, testing, and managing Rust projects. Cargo is the backbone of the system. Many of the tasks that are associated with managing a Rust project can be automated with this tool, which makes it an indispensable tool for developers.

The following is a more in-depth understanding of Cargo and its functionalities:

Cargo's Key Features

Crate Dependencies Management

Cargo simplifies how dependencies are handled in Rust projects. By specifying your project's dependencies in a **Cargo.toml** file, Cargo automatically handles downloading, building, and compiling these dependencies, ensuring that your project always has the necessary libraries it needs to run and build correctly. This file acts as a manifest and is central to defining both your project settings and dependencies.

Build Automation

One of Cargo's standout features is its ability to automate the building of projects. With a simple command (**cargo build**), Cargo compiles your entire project along with its dependencies. This automation extends to watching for changes in your project's files, intelligently determining what needs to be recompiled, thereby saving time and computational resources.

Testing Facilitation

Testing is integral to developing robust software, and Cargo supports this with its built-in commands. By running **cargo test**, you can execute all unit, documentation, and integration tests associated with your project, making it easier to maintain code quality and functionality throughout the development lifecycle.

Documentation Generation

Cargo also aids in generating documentation for your project directly from your code's annotations. By using **cargo doc**, you can create HTML documentation for your project and all installed dependencies, making it accessible through a web browser and easy to navigate.

Package Publishing

Cargo connects directly to crates.io, Rust's package registry, allowing you to publish your libraries and make them available to the Rust community. The **cargo publish** command streamlines the process of updating and distributing your packages, enforcing version checks and dependency validations to ensure compatibility and stability.

Sample Program

To put these concepts into practice, we now consider a simple Rust project managed by Cargo. In this project, you might have a **Cargo.toml** file that looks like this:

```
[package]

name = "my_project"

version = "0.1.0"
```

```
edition = "2018"


[dependencies]

serde = "1.0"
```

This file declares the project as a package with a name and a version, and it specifies **serde** as a dependency. When you run **cargo build**, Cargo checks this file, downloads the serde library if it isn't already present, and compiles your project along with the dependency.

Crates Basics

Crates are the building blocks of software, acting as executables to carry out particular tasks or libraries to provide reusable functionality. Successful Rust programmers have a firm grasp on the language's two primary crates, binary and library.

Binary Crates

Binary crates are those that compile into executables. These crates must contain a **main** function, which serves as the entry point for the program. When you run **cargo build** on a binary crate, Cargo compiles it into a binary executable, which you can then run directly from the command line.

Library Crates

Library crates, on the other hand, provide specific functionalities that can be used by other Rust programs but do not compile into executables themselves. These crates do not have a **main** function; instead, they consist of a set of functions, types, modules, and traits that can be integrated into other Rust projects. Library crates are typically used as dependencies within other projects.

Sample Program: Using a Crate

To illustrate how to use a crate in a Rust project, we consider a common library crate: **rand**, which is used for generating random numbers.

First, you would add **rand** to your **Cargo.toml** file under the **[dependencies]** section:

```
[dependencies]
```

```
rand = "0.8.0"
```

Next, in your Rust source file, you can use the **rand** crate to generate a random number:

```
use rand::Rng; // Import the Rng trait to use its methods


fn main() {

 let mut rng = rand::thread_rng(); // Create a random
number generator

 let n: u32 = rng.gen(); // Generate a random number

 println!("Random number: {}", n);

}
```

In the above sample program, **rand::thread_rng()** creates a new random number generator, and **rng.gen()** generates a random number of type **u32**. Cargo helps in building, testing, and documenting your projects, as well as publishing them to **crates.io**, the Rust community's package registry.

Understanding Packages

To effectively manage and organise your code, the idea of a package is foundational. You can organise one or more crates—library crates, binary crates, or both—into a coherent whole along with all the necessary configuration details by creating a package, which is basically a Cargo project.

Key Components of a Rust Package

Cargo.toml

This is the configuration file where you define your package. It includes metadata such as the package name, version, authors, and dependencies. You also specify which crates are included in the package.

src Folder

This contains the source files for the crate or crates. The main file for a binary crate is typically **main.rs**, while for a library crate, it's **lib.rs**.

Target Directory

This is where the output of compiled binaries and other artifacts are stored.

Creating and Configuring a Package

To create a package, you generally start by generating a new project using Cargo:

```
cargo new my_package
```

This command creates a new directory called **my_package** with the initial file structure, including a **Cargo.toml** file at its root. The generated **Cargo.toml** file might look like this:

```
[package]

name = "my_package"

version = "0.1.0"

authors = ["Your Name <you@gitforgits.com>"]

edition = "2018"



[dependencies]
```

In this file:

- The **[package]** section defines the package's name, version, authors, and the Rust edition.

- The **[dependencies]** section is used to list other crates on which your package depends.

Sample Program: Using Package and Adding Dependency

Suppose you want to add a dependency to a popular crate, such as **serde**, for handling serialization. You would update your **Cargo.toml** file like this:

```
[dependencies]

serde = "1.0"
```

This tells Cargo to download and build **serde**, making it available to your project.

Within your package's source files, you can use the functionalities provided by your dependencies. For instance, in **main.rs** or **lib.rs**, you could start using **serde** by adding:

```
extern crate serde;


fn main() {

 // Your code using serde here

}
```

Using packages in Rust has several benefits:

- Packages help keep related components together, making code easier to navigate and maintain.

- By splitting functionality into packages, you can easily reuse code across multiple projects.

- Cargo handles downloading, building, and linking your dependencies automatically.

Cargo vs Crates vs Packages

Cargo

Cargo is Rust's package manager and build system. Cargo is the tool you use to orchestrate the building of your project, handle external libraries, and ensure that your project compiles with all its dependencies correctly. It uses a file called **Cargo.toml** to manage these configurations.

Its primary roles include:

- Compiling projects: Cargo compiles both binary and library crates.

- Managing dependencies: It automatically downloads and compiles your project's dependencies.

- Running tests and building documentation: Cargo provides commands for running tests (**`cargo test`**) and building documentation (**`cargo doc`**).

- Publishing libraries: It assists in publishing your libraries to **`crates.io`**, the official Rust package registry.

Crates

A crate is the smallest amount of code that the Rust compiler considers at a time. Crates can be published to **`crates.io`** and shared with other Rust users. They encapsulate functionality in a way that promotes reusability and modular code design.

Crates come in two types:

- Library crates: These provide reusable functionality to other programs. They do not have a **`main`** function and cannot compile into a standalone executable.

- Binary crates: These compile into executables and are runnable programs. They have a **`main`** function that serves as the entry point of the program.

Packages

A package is a feature of Cargo that lets you build, test, and share crates. A package might contain multiple binary crates and optionally one library crate. Each crate in a package can be run or tested separately, and they can depend on each other.

A package:

- Contains at least one crate (library or binary).

- Has a **`Cargo.toml`** file at its root, which describes how to build those crates.

- Can include multiple crates but often contains just one.

Together, these components make Rust's ecosystem highly modular and maintainable, with Cargo managing the compilation and packaging process, crates providing the building blocks, and packages organizing these blocks within a configurable project structure.

Creating My First Crate

The initial step in making your first crate in Rust is to utilize Cargo, which is both a build system and a package manager. The following is a much better example of creating a library crate. For name sake, we label it as "helpcode".

Sample Program: Creating a Library Crate

Creating the Crate

To create a new library crate, you use the **cargo new** command with the **--lib** flag. This specifies that the project is a library, not a binary executable. Given below is how you do it:

```
cargo new helpcode --lib
```

This command creates a directory called "helpcode" containing the necessary basic structure for a library crate.

Project Structure

Inside the **helpcode** directory, Cargo generates a few essential files such as cargo.toml and src/lib.rs.

The directory structure will look like this:

```
helpcode/
├── Cargo.toml
└── src/
    └── lib.rs
```

Developing Your Crate

Begin by adding your Rust code into the **src/lib.rs** file. This could include functions, types, and constants that define the functionality of your crate. You can also create more modules within the **src** directory to keep your code organized and modular.

Navigate to your crate directory in the terminal and run:

```
cargo build
```

This compiles your crate and any dependencies, ensuring that the crate is ready to use or publish.

Testing and Document

If you've written tests (highly recommended), run them using:

```
cargo test
```

This helps ensure your crate functions as expected before you publish or share it. Automatically generate documentation by running:

```
cargo doc --open
```

This generates HTML documentation from your code comments and opens it in your web browser.

Publishing the Crate

Once your crate is tested and documented, you can publish it to crates.io with:

```
cargo publish
```

This command packages up your crate and uploads it, making it available for others to use in their projects.

Best Practices

1. Do not forget to document your functions and modules using Rust's documentation comments (e.g., **///** or **//!**) to provide users and contributors with clear guidance on how your crate works.

2. Follow semantic versioning rules when updating your crate to help users understand the impact of incorporating a new version into their projects.

3. Develop comprehensive tests for your functions to ensure your crate's reliability and robustness.

By following the steps and practices outlined above, you can create, develop, and maintain a Rust crate that benefits the Rust ecosystem while also enhancing your developer portfolio.

Build My First Package

Following is an updated version of the build process for Rust packages, along with some extra tips for managing the build process efficiently.

Basic Build

To compile your package along with all its dependencies, navigate to your project's root directory (where the **Cargo.toml** file is located) and run:

```
cargo build
```

This command compiles your project in debug mode by default, placing the compiled output in the **target/debug** directory. This mode includes debugging information that helps you diagnose errors in your code but doesn't optimize the compilation.

Release Build

When you are ready to deploy your application or when you need to benchmark its performance, build your package in release mode:

```
cargo build --release
```

This compiles your project with optimizations enabled, improving performance but taking a bit longer to compile. The output is stored in **target/release**.

Checking Build Feasibility₹

If you want to quickly check whether your code compiles without actually producing an executable, you can use:

```
cargo check
```

This command runs much faster than **cargo build** because it skips the step of producing an executable. It's useful for rapid iterations when you are writing and testing new code.

Understanding the Build Output

After running **cargo build**, Cargo outputs binaries, libraries, and other types of artifacts depending on your project type (binary or library). These outputs are stored in the **target/debug** or **target/release** directory based on the build mode you chose.

Debugging Build Issues

Cargo provides detailed error messages when builds fail. It points to the precise location in your code that caused the issue, which can include syntax errors, type mismatches, missing functions, or unresolved crates and modules. Carefully read these error messages as they often provide guidance on how to resolve the issue.

Incremental Compilation

Rust supports incremental compilation, which means that subsequent builds after the first one are faster because Cargo only recompiles the parts of your project that have changed since the last build. This feature significantly speeds up the development process.

Package and Dependency Management

The **Cargo.toml** file is crucial for managing dependencies. Here you specify which crates your project depends on, and Cargo handles downloading, updating, and compiling these dependencies. Following is a sample dependency entry:

```
[dependencies]

serde = "1.0"
```

This line tells Cargo to download and use the **serde** crate version 1.0.

By constructing your initial Rust package with Cargo, you will gain a solid grounding in the language's application management and compilation capabilities, as well as an understanding of how to make the most of Rust's robust cargo ecosystem.

Publish the Package

One of the first steps in making your work available to the wider Rust community is publishing a package to crates.io. To help you publish your crate using Cargo, the package manager in Rust, given below is a more in-depth preparatory steps:

Cargo.toml Configuration

Ensure that your **Cargo.toml** file is accurately filled out. This includes specifying the package name, version, authors, and other metadata. It's crucial because this information will be displayed on crates.io and will be used by others to find your crate.

Given below is an example of what your **Cargo.toml** might look like:

```
[package]

name = "helpcode"

version = "0.1.0"

authors = ["Alice <alice@gitforgits.com>"]
```

```
description = "A helpful utility library for Rust
developers."

license = "MIT"


[dependencies]

serde = "1.0"
```

Documentation and Readme

Ensure you have a **README.md** file in your project root. This file should explain what your crate does, how to use it, and any other relevant information.

You should also include inline documentation in your Rust files using **///** for doc comments. Cargo can automatically generate user documentation from these comments with the **cargo doc** command.

Authentication

Before you can publish, you must authenticate with crates.io. First, create an account on crates.io if you haven't already.

Then use the **cargo login** command along with your API token from crates.io:

```
cargo login your_api_token_here
```

This token links your local development environment with your account on crates.io, ensuring that you are authorized to publish updates.

Testing and Validation

Run **cargo test** to ensure all tests pass without any issues, ensuring your crate works as expected.

It's also good practice to check that your package compiles with no warnings or errors using **cargo build** and **cargo check**.

Versioning

Follow semantic versioning rules (**major.minor.patch**). If you make backward-compatible changes, increment the minor or patch version. If your changes break compatibility, increment the major version.

Publishing the Crate

Once you've completed the preparation steps, you are ready to publish. Use the **cargo publish** command. This will compile your crate, package it up, and upload it to crates.io:

```
cargo publish
```

If you have large files or optional features, consider using the **--no-verify** flag to skip the local package verification step:

```
cargo publish --no-verify
```

Post-Publication

Your crate is now publicly available on crates.io after publishing, so anyone can use it as a dependency in their own projects.

Keep an eye on your crate to watch for pull requests or issues. If you want your crate to stay healthy and evolve, you need to engage with users who report issues or make suggestions.

Following these detailed steps and considerations will allow you to effectively manage your Rust crate's lifecycle from creation to publication, ensuring that it is well-received and useful to the Rust community.

Role of Modules and Paths

When working on bigger projects, modules and paths are essential for code organization and scope management. You can improve code readability, maintainability, and functionality encapsulation by using paths and modules effectively.

Understanding Modules in Rust

Modules are declared using the **mod** keyword, and they serve as containers for other items like functions, structs, enums, or even other modules. This encapsulation helps in logically grouping related functionalities, which is especially useful in larger codebases. For example:

```
mod my_module {
```

```
pub fn foo() {

println!("This is a function inside my_module.");

}
```

In the above code snippet, **my_module** contains a function **foo**. Notice the use of **pub** before **fn**, which makes the function public and thus accessible from outside the module.

Using 'use' Keyword

To simplify access to items within modules, Rust provides the **use** keyword, allowing you to bring items into scope. This reduces redundancy in your code and makes it cleaner and more manageable:

```
mod my_module {

 pub fn foo() {

 println!("This is a function inside my_module.");

 }

}


use my_module::foo;


fn main() {

 foo(); // Directly use foo() thanks to the `use`
statement.

}
```

Nested Modules

Modules can be nested within each other, forming a tree-like hierarchy. This is useful for further organizing your code into a logical structure:

```rust
mod my_lib {

 pub mod module_a {

 pub fn foo() {

 println!("Function foo from module_a.");

 }

 }


 pub mod module_b {

 pub fn bar() {

 println!("Function bar from module_b.");

 }

 }

}


use my_lib::module_a::foo;


fn main() {

 foo(); // Using foo() from module_a

}
```

Understanding Paths

Paths are used to refer to an item within the module structure. They can be absolute or relative. Absolute paths start from a crate root by using a crate name or a literal **crate**. Relative paths start from the current module and use **self**, **super**, or an identifier in the current module.

Following is how you might use paths to access functions or structs:

```
mod my_module {

 pub struct MyStruct {

 pub field: i32,

 }

}


use crate::my_module::MyStruct;


fn main() {

 let instance = MyStruct { field: 123 };

 println!("Field value: {}", instance.field);

}
```

When developers make good use of modules and paths, they are able to keep their organizational structure clear, which facilitates navigating complicated projects, refactoring code, and managing visibility and scope. Not only does this method lend itself to more effective code management practices, but it also improves teamwork in settings where transparency and consistency are paramount.

Summary

Cargo, crates, and packages are fundamental to Rust project management and structure, and we explored their inner workings in this chapter. You can build code, manage dependencies, run tests, and publish packages to crates.io with the help of Cargo, the built-in package manager in Rust.

The building blocks of Rust, called crates, can be either binary files or libraries.

The idea of packages allowed for the construction, execution, and testing of multiple crates that shared a Cargo.toml file. Developers were able to efficiently organize and distribute Rust code with this setup. We also delved into Rust's module and path hierarchies, which can be used to efficiently organize and encapsulate code. For large codebases, this structure is essential for maintenance because it makes them easier to navigate and manage. Paths allow you to find and refer to these functionalities within the project or external crates, while modules help group related functionalities.

Not only that, but we learned the ins and outs of making a crate and package, which demonstrated how to start a project, oversee its construction, and get it ready for publication. The importance of metadata and version management was highlighted as the process of publishing a crate to crates.io was demonstrated, highlighting how the crate can be useful and accessible to other developers.

This chapter laid a solid groundwork for creating strong Rust applications and libraries by providing a playful introduction to the language's powerful package management and project structuring tools.

CHAPTER 8: CARGO COMMANDS

Introduction

In this chapter, we'll explore the expansive set of commands offered by Cargo, the package manager for Rust. Because it simplifies activities like project building, package management, and deployment, cargo is a must-have for Rust developers. In this chapter, you'll learn about the spectrum of Cargo commands, categorized into several key areas:

- General Commands: These commands cover basic functionalities like starting new projects or checking the compilability of code without producing an executable.

- Build Commands: You'll explore how to compile your projects, run tests, and generate documentation, ensuring your Rust applications are ready for production.

- Package Commands: This section will teach you through managing dependencies, updating crates, and handling other package-related tasks to maintain the health and currency of your projects.

- Manifest Commands: Since the manifest file (**Cargo.toml**) is crucial for defining your package's settings, you'll learn how to manipulate and understand this file's configurations.

- Publish Commands: Learn the steps to package and distribute your libraries to **crates.io**, making your work available to the Rust community.

- Custom Commands: Finally, the flexibility of Cargo allows you to extend its functionality. This part will introduce you to creating custom commands tailored to your project's needs.

Gaining command over these commands will equip you to optimize and manage your Rust development process, leading to a more productive and error-free coding workflow.

General Commands

In this section, we will go over the fundamental Cargo commands and how to use them in a typical Rust project workflow. We will also provide examples that correspond to our previous chapters.

Creating and Initializing Projects

When starting a new Rust project, you can use either **cargo new** or **cargo init** depending on whether you are starting in a new directory or an existing one.

For example:

If we recall our previous learning on setting up a new project for demonstrating ownership and borrowing:

```
cargo new ownership_project
```

This command creates a new directory called **ownership_project** with a basic Rust setup, including a **Cargo.toml** and a **src/main.rs** file.

If you already have a directory and want to initialize a Rust project in it:

```
cd existing_directory

cargo init
```

This sets up Rust project files within **existing_directory** without creating a new folder.

Checking and Building Projects

For quick checks to ensure your code compiles without generating an executable:

```
cargo check
```

This is especially useful when incrementally building complex features like the module and path system learned earlier, allowing for fast validation of changes without full compilation.

To compile the project and see the full output:

```
cargo build
```

This command compiles all source files into an executable in **target/debug**. For instance, after adding a new function to calculate borrowing costs in a financial application, you'd run this to ensure everything compiles.

Running Projects

To run the executable directly through Cargo, which is particularly handy during development for immediate feedback:

```
cargo run
```

Imagine we have a completed function in **src/main.rs** that demonstrates the use of enums in error handling, as learned in the enums chapter. Running this command would compile (if necessary) and execute the main function.

Testing Projects

For running tests defined in your Rust code:

```
cargo test
```

This command is crucial after modifications or additions, such as when we introduced new functionality in our crate and needed to ensure existing features were not adversely affected.

Cleaning up Build Files

To clean up the project by removing the **target** directory that holds build files and artifacts:

```
cargo clean
```

Use this after a series of builds to clean up the workspace, which can help in cases where old artifacts cause issues.

Viewing Documentation Locally

To generate and view documentation for your project and all dependencies:

```
cargo doc --open
```

This could be used to check the documentation comments added to our public functions, ensuring they are correctly formatted and informative.

The daily activities in Rust development revolve around these commands, which help manage the project's lifecycle from creation to execution. As stated in the Cargo.toml and source files, each command interacts with the project structure and configuration.

Build Commands

Cargo offers several commands under the build category, each tailored for different stages of development, from compiling to optimizing.

cargo build

This command compiles the current project and all of its dependencies. It's the basic command you use to ensure that your code compiles correctly.

For example:

In our earlier learning about creating a new crate for handling HTTP requests, you'd run the following command after adding new functionality or making changes to the source files:

```
cargo build
```

This would compile the project in debug mode, which is useful for development since it includes debugging information and does not apply optimizations, making compile times faster and debugging easier.

cargo build --release

When you are ready to deploy your application or need to benchmark its performance, you compile it in release mode. This command compiles the project with optimizations, improving performance but taking longer to compile.

For example:

For the financial application on calculating loan interest, compiling in release mode before deployment ensures it runs efficiently as below:

```
cargo build --release
```

This command generates the executable in **target/release**, optimized for performance.

cargo check

This command quickly checks your code to ensure it compiles but doesn't produce an executable. It's a faster way to catch errors during development.

For example:

When we added error handling using enums and match expressions, running this command:

```
cargo check
```

would allow you to verify that all branches are handled correctly without the wait time associated with a full build.

cargo clean

After many builds, your project's target directory can become cluttered with build artifacts. To clean up:

```
cargo clean
```

This would remove the **target** directory, clearing all compiled files and artifacts, which is useful for ensuring that your next build is clean from any past build residues.

At its heart, managing a Rust project's build process are these commands, which guarantee efficient code writing, compilation, optimization, and maintenance.

Manifest Commands

Cargo's manifest commands are used to manage and interact with the **Cargo.toml** file in a Rust project. The **Cargo.toml** file is where you define various aspects of your project, including dependencies, metadata, and configurations.

cargo metadata

This command outputs detailed information about the current package in a JSON format, including dependencies, versions, and more. This is particularly useful for developers needing to automate tooling or integrate with other systems.

For example:

Suppose we've been working on a library crate for parsing financial transactions. Running **cargo metadata** could help you extract and use metadata programmatically, for instance, in a script that checks dependency versions or integrates with a documentation generation tool.

cargo pkgid

This command helps identify the package identifier for the current package or the specified package. It's useful when you need to specify a particular version of a package precisely in commands or scripts.

For example:

In our previous learnings about modules and paths, if you wanted to ensure you are working with the correct version of a crate used in the project, you could use:

```
cargo pkgid
```

This would output the pkgid which can be used in Cargo commands where specifying the package version is necessary, like when updating a dependency to a new version.

cargo tree

This command displays a tree visualization of a project's dependencies. It's an invaluable tool for understanding how different crates relate to each other, and for identifying potential conflicts or redundancies.

For example:

For the Rust project that handles HTTP requests, using **cargo tree** can help you visualize how the **hyper** crate might depend on other crates like **tokio** and **futures**, providing a clear view of the dependency graph.

cargo vendor

This command vendors all dependencies for a project into the **vendor/** directory. This is especially useful for ensuring all dependencies are locally available, for example in a build environment without internet access.

For example:

In the context of our learnings about efficient Cargo management, if you were preparing to build your financial application in an environment where internet access is restricted, you could use:

```
cargo vendor
```

This would copy all required dependencies locally, allowing the build process to proceed without needing to fetch crates from the internet.

In complex or enterprise-level environments, where automation and precise control over dependencies are required, these manifest commands play a crucial role in Rust programs.

Package and Publish Commands

To prepare and distribute your Rust packages, you must use Cargo's package and publish commands. The following are a few additional, far more important commands that any rust programmer should know:

cargo package

This command packages your library or application into a format that can be published to crates.io, or shared as a local package. It essentially compiles the crate and then packs it together with all of its dependencies and metadata into a **.crate** file.

For example:

Consider our library crate developed for parsing financial transactions. To prepare this crate for publication, you would first run:

```
cargo package
```

This command verifies that the crate can be packaged without any issues, compiles the crate, and then packages it. The output includes a path to the generated **.crate** file, which you can then inspect to ensure everything is packaged as expected.

cargo publish

This command uploads the package to crates.io, making it publicly available to other developers. Before you can publish, you must be logged in with a valid crates.io account.

For example:

Once your financial parsing library is tested and packaged, you might decide to share it with the Rust community. First, ensure you are logged in:

```
cargo login [your-token-here]
```

Then, you publish your crate:

```
cargo publish
```

This uploads the packaged **.crate** file to crates.io. If the crate has dependencies that aren't yet on crates.io, the command will give an error, prompting you to publish those dependencies first.

Custom Commands

In Cargo tool, custom commands extend Cargo's functionality, allowing developers or teams to integrate additional tools or scripts directly into the Cargo workflow. These commands can be particularly useful for automating tasks, enforcing coding standards, or integrating with other software development tools.

Creating Custom Commands

Custom commands in Cargo are external executables that Cargo recognizes by prefixing them with **cargo-**. When you name a program **cargo-something**, Cargo will allow you to execute it via **cargo something**. This executable needs to be in your system's PATH for Cargo to invoke it.

For example:

Consider that we need to create a custom command to automate the cleanup of debug files generated during development. You might create a script named **cargo-cleanup**. This script could be a simple Bash script on a Unix-like system or a batch file on Windows.

Following is the script setup:

- File Name: cargo-cleanup

- Location: Any directory included in your system's PATH.

Following is the sample script:

```
#!/bin/sh

echo "Cleaning up debug files..."

rm -rf target/debug/*.d
```

To use this script, you would simply call it via Cargo:

```
cargo cleanup
```

Deploying Custom Commands

To make a custom Cargo command available:

- Ensure the script is executable. On Unix-like systems, you would use **chmod +x cargo-cleanup**.

- Place the script in a directory that is on your system's PATH or add its directory to the PATH.

- For team environments, you might distribute the script via an internal tooling repository or include it in your project's repository and recommend developers add the directory to their PATH.

Integrating with Build Processes

Custom commands can be integrated into your build or CI/CD processes for additional checks or automation steps. For instance, you might create a command like **cargo-check-style** to integrate with a code style checker or linter.

Consider you have a complex Rust project and you want to ensure all contributors run tests and lint checks before pushing code. You could create a script **cargo-prepush** that runs these checks and then instruct your team to run:

before each push to the repository. This can enforce a consistent code quality standard across your team.

These custom commands let you tailor Cargo to your specific project needs, promoting more efficient and standardized development practices.

Summary

This chapter explored the use of Cargo commands in managing Rust projects in detail. It all began with the introduction of some basic commands, like cargo new, which allowed users to create new projects, and cargo run, which allowed users to directly compile and run the Rust application. Next, we moved on to the topic of build commands, which are essential when putting together projects that have debugging or release optimization options. To build and verify code without producing executables, commands like cargo build and cargo check are highlighted.

Also covered in this chapter were the manifest commands, with a focus on the cargo metadata and cargo tree that reveal the package's dependency hierarchies and structure in great detail. After making sure all the configurations are set up correctly in Cargo.toml, the complex process of publishing is covered under publish commands. It shows how to use cargo publish to distribute crates to crates.io.

Furthermore, the chapter clarified the notion of custom commands, a sophisticated capability that grants developers the freedom to craft their very own Cargo commands tailored to particular automation tasks or workflows. For tailored development procedures, these commands are crucial because they increase adaptability and fit in with Rust's environment perfectly.

By providing examples that relate to common development tasks, this chapter helps you to grasp not just the syntax but also how each command is used in real-world programming situations.

CHAPTER 9: RUST STANDARD LIBRARY

Introduction

In Chapter 9, we explore the Rust Standard Library, a big collection of features that help with common computation, data manipulation, and interaction tasks in Rust. If you want to know how to use the library properly across all of its modules and features, this chapter is for you to succeed.

We start by exploring the overall structure of the Rust Standard Library, highlighting its most popular modules. These modules cover a range of functionalities from system handling to algorithm implementation, providing a solid foundation for building robust applications.

Next, the topics focuses on primitive types. Rust's approach to basic data types is nuanced, offering more control and safety features compared to many other languages. Understanding these types can aid in writing more efficient and safer code.

The chapter also covers collections extensively. Rust offers several collections types like vectors, hash maps, and others that are optimized for performance and safety, ensuring that data handling is both flexible and secure.

Macros, another powerful feature of Rust, are learned in detail. They allow for writing more dynamic and reusable code snippets. The chapter will not only explain what macros are but also teach you through writing your first macro, demonstrating how to automate repetitive tasks and extend the language's capabilities.

This comprehensive overview provides the tools and knowledge to leverage the Rust Standard Library effectively, enhancing both the breadth and depth of your Rust programming skills.

Rust Standard Library (std)

The Rust Standard Library, commonly referred to as **std**, is a comprehensive suite that supports the Rust programming language, providing essential functionality across various domains to facilitate effective and safe programming practices.

Modules and Functionalities

- Collections (**std::collections**): This module offers various data structures such as **Vec**, **HashMap**, and **LinkedList**, optimizing data storage and operations to accommodate different use cases efficiently.

- Error Handling (**std::error**): It provides traits and implementations for error handling, facilitating a robust way to manage and report errors within applications.

- File System Operations (**std::fs**): Functions for interacting with the file system, including file creation, reading, writing, and metadata management, are found here, making file handling straightforward and secure.

- Input/Output (**std::io**): This module includes traits and classes for input and output operations, both synchronous and asynchronous, allowing for flexible data exchange with the external environment.

- Networking (**std::net**): It covers the creation and management of network sockets, enabling the development of networked applications with TCP and UDP protocols.

- Concurrency (**std::sync**): With tools like mutexes, channels, and atomic counters, this module supports safe and efficient concurrent programming.

- Time and Date (**std::time**): It provides functionality for measuring and manipulating time, dates, and durations, essential for time-based operations in applications.

The Rust Standard Library is designed with Rust's philosophy of safety and performance. It uses Rust's ownership and type systems to prevent common bugs such as null/dangling pointer dereferences and data races. Moreover, each element of the library is thoroughly documented, offering clear guidance and examples that are accessible via Rust's official documentation website.

std::collections

Exploring the **std::collections::HashMap** further showcases its robustness and flexibility for handling key-value data. Given below is a comprehensive look at using a **HashMap**, focusing on its various methods and how they can be applied to practical problems:

Initialization and Insertion

A **HashMap** can be created and populated with initial values using the **insert** method. Given below is how you would typically start by initializing a **HashMap** and adding some key-value pairs:

```
use std::collections::HashMap;


let mut map = HashMap::new();

map.insert("key1", 10);

map.insert("key2", 20);
```

Accessing Values

To access values, **HashMap** offers the **get** method, which returns an **Option**. This means it will return **Some(&value)** if the key exists or **None** if it does not. This approach ensures that accessing values is always safe and doesn't result in a panic:

```
if let Some(value) = map.get("key1") {

 println!("Value: {}", value);

} else {

 println!("Key not found.");

}
```

Updating Entries

HashMap allows you to update the value associated with a specific key directly or use more sophisticated methods like **entry()** combined with **or_insert()** which provides a powerful way to only insert a value if the key does not already exist:

```
*map.entry("key2").or_insert(0) += 30;
```

This code checks for the existence of **"key2"** and either updates its value by adding 30 or inserts **0** and then adds 30 if it was not there initially.

Handling Missing Entries

For cases where a key might not exist, and you need to handle its absence, Rust's **entry()** API is particularly useful. It allows for elegant handling of absent keys with default values:

```
let count = map.entry("key3").or_insert(0);

*count += 1;
```

Iteration

Iterating over a **HashMap** allows you to access each key-value pair. Rust ensures that this process is straightforward and efficient:

```
for (key, value) in map.iter() {

 println!("{}: {}", key, value);
```

```
}
```

Sample Program

A common use case for **HashMap** is counting the frequency of elements, such as words in text data:

```
let text = "hello world hello";

let mut word_count = HashMap::new();


for word in text.split_whitespace() {

 let count = word_count.entry(word).or_insert(0);

 *count += 1;

}

println!("{:?}", word_count); // Outputs: {"hello": 2,
"world": 1}
```

This snippet efficiently counts the occurrences of each word, demonstrating **HashMap**'s capability to manage data where quick access and updates are necessary.

To sum up, **std::collections::HashMap** provides a rich set of functionalities that are crucial for efficient data handling and manipulation in Rust, making it an indispensable tool for developers.

std::error

The **std::error** module plays a crucial role in facilitating effective error handling across different components of your programs. Specifically, it provides the **Error** trait, which any error type can implement, making it easier to handle errors uniformly. Understanding how to leverage this module, especially in conjunction with **std::result**, can greatly enhance the reliability and maintainability of your Rust applications.

Simplifying Error Handling

A typical use case involves performing file operations where errors might occur, such as attempting to read from a file that doesn't exist or isn't accessible. Rust's approach encourages the use of **Result** types to handle such conditions gracefully without crashing the program (as opposed to using panic-inducing methods like **unwrap()**).

Sample Program

Given below is an example of refined error handling while reading a file:

```rust
use std::fs;

use std::io::{self, Read};


fn read_file(filename: &str) -> io::Result<String> {

  fs::read_to_string(filename)

}


fn main() {

 match read_file("my_file.txt") {

 Ok(contents) => println!("File contents: {}", contents),

 Err(e) => println!("Failed to read file: {}", e),

 }

}
```

In the above sample program,

- The **read_file** function leverages **fs::read_to_string** to attempt to read the entire contents of a file into a **String**. This function returns an **io::Result<String>**, which is a specialized version of **Result** specifically designed for I/O operations.

- Using **match** in the **main** function allows us to handle both possible outcomes of the **read_file** function:
    - o If **read_file** returns **Ok(contents)**, the contents of the file are printed.
    - o If **read_file** returns **Err(e)**, the error message is printed, indicating why the file couldn't be read.

This approach not only makes your code more robust by safely handling potential errors but also improves its readability and maintainability by clearly outlining the possible outcomes of functions that might fail.

std::net

The **std::net** module provides functionality for network programming, including the ability to handle TCP and UDP sockets. This module is essential for writing network applications such as web servers or clients, TCP servers, or UDP services.

Given below is how you might use **std::net** to build a basic TCP server:

Setting up a Listener

You start by creating a **TcpListener**. This binds to a specific socket address and listens for incoming TCP connections.

```
let listener = TcpListener::bind("127.0.0.1:8080")?;
```

Handling Incoming Connections

The listener's **incoming()** method returns an iterator over the incoming connections. For each connection, you get a **TcpStream**, which represents a client connection.

```
for stream in listener.incoming() {

 match stream {

 Ok(mut stream) => {

 // Handle the connection

 }

 Err(e) => { /* connection failed */ }
```

```
    }
}
```

Reading and Writing

Once you have a **TcpStream**, you can read from and write to it. Reading from a stream typically involves specifying a buffer into which data will be read.

```
let mut buf = [0; 1024];

stream.read(&mut buf)?;
```

Responding to Clients

After processing the request, you can write a response back to the client using the same stream.

```
let response = "HTTP/1.1 200 OK\r\n\r\nHello, world!";

stream.write_all(response.as_bytes())?;

stream.flush()?;
```

Error Handling

Proper error handling is crucial. Using **?** instead of **unwrap()** helps prevent the server from panicking and crashing when an error occurs. It's better to log the error or handle it gracefully.

Sample Program

Suppose you want to implement a simple HTTP server. Given below is a condensed version of how it might look, handling basic HTTP GET requests:

```
use std::io::prelude::*;

use std::net::{TcpListener, TcpStream};


fn handle_connection(mut stream: TcpStream) ->
std::io::Result<()> {
```

```
  let mut buffer = [0; 1024];

  stream.read(&mut buffer)?;

  let response = "HTTP/1.1 200 OK\r\nContent-Length:
13\r\n\r\nHello, world!";

  stream.write_all(response.as_bytes())?;

  stream.flush()?;

  Ok(())

}


fn main() -> std::io::Result<()> {

  let listener = TcpListener::bind("127.0.0.1:8080")?;

  for stream in listener.incoming() {

  if let Ok(stream) = stream {

  handle_connection(stream)?;

  }

  }

  Ok(())

}
```

In this code, each connection is handled by reading data into a buffer, then sending a simple HTTP response. This basic server can be expanded with more complex routing, error handling, and multi-threading to handle multiple connections simultaneously.

By using **std::net**, Rust provides a robust foundation for network programming, leveraging Rust's performance and safety features to build efficient and secure network applications.

std::sync

The **std::sync** module is essential for safe concurrency, ensuring data consistency and preventing race conditions. This module contains several primitives, such as **Mutex**, **Arc**, and **RwLock**, each serving specific threading needs.

Arc and Mutex

Arc (Atomic Reference Counting) is a thread-safe reference-counting pointer, used when data needs to be accessed by multiple threads. **Mutex** (Mutual Exclusion), on the other hand, is used to guard data with exclusive access, ensuring that only one thread can access the data at a time by locking and unlocking the data.

Sample Program

Consider a scenario where you need to safely increment a shared integer from multiple threads:

```rust
use std::sync::{Arc, Mutex};

use std::thread;


fn main() {

 // Initialize Arc wrapping a Mutex that guards an integer

 let counter = Arc::new(Mutex::new(0));


 // Vector to hold the handles of the spawned threads

 let mut handles = vec![];


 for _ in 0..10 {

 // Clone the Arc to have multiple owners
```

```rust
    let counter_clone = Arc::clone(&counter);


    // Create a new thread
    let handle = thread::spawn(move || {
    // Lock the Mutex to gain access to the data
    let mut num = counter_clone.lock().unwrap();
    // Modify the data
    *num += 1;
    });


    handles.push(handle);
    }


    // Wait for all threads to complete
    for handle in handles {
    handle.join().unwrap();
    }


    // Safely access the data and print the result
    println!("Result: {}", *counter.lock().unwrap());
}
```

In the above sample program,

- Arc enables multiple threads to own the same data; necessary where ownership needs to be shared.

- Mutex provides mutually exclusive access to data. When a thread wants to modify the data, it must first lock the mutex.

- Threads access data by first calling the **lock** method, which blocks until the lock is acquired. The returned guard can be dereferenced to access the data.

- The lock is released if a panic occurs, preventing deadlocks.

- It's crucial to join threads to ensure that all operations complete before the main thread exits, avoiding premature termination of the program.

std::time

The **std::time** module provides powerful tools for handling time operations, like measuring durations or working with system time. This module is crucial for any operations where tracking time or measuring the duration of events is necessary.

Key Components

- SystemTime: This is used to represent an instant in time, typically measured from the system's clock. It's commonly used for timestamps and measuring durations.

- Instant: Similar to **SystemTime**, but provides a monotonic clock source. **Instant** is best used for measuring durations in a consistent manner, without the risk of adjustments from the system clock.

- Duration: Represents a span of time. It is commonly used to calculate differences between instances of **SystemTime** or **Instant**.

Sample Program

Given below is a demonstration of how to use **SystemTime** to measure how long a block of code takes to execute:

```
use std::time::{SystemTime, Duration};



fn main() {
```

```
let start_time = SystemTime::now(); // Capture the start
time


// Example workload: Calculate sum of first 10,000
integers

let sum: u32 = (1..10000).sum();


// Check the elapsed time

if let Ok(elapsed) =
SystemTime::now().duration_since(start_time) {

println!("Time taken: {} seconds", elapsed.as_secs());

println!("Sum: {}", sum);

} else {

println!("Failed to measure time.");

}

}
```

Key Concepts

- **SystemTime::now()**: Captures the current system time.

- **duration_since()**: Calculates the duration between two **SystemTime** instances, returning a **Result** type that may need to be handled for errors (e.g., if the system clock changes).

- **as_secs()** and **as_millis()**: Converts a **Duration** into seconds or milliseconds, respectively.

This above example demonstrates using **SystemTime** to measure the execution time of a function or any block of code, providing useful metrics for performance monitoring or optimization.

std::env

The **std::env** module provides functionality to interact with the execution environment of the program, including working with environment variables, command-line arguments, and other aspects of its environment.

Key Functions

- **args()**: This function returns an iterator that allows you to access the raw command-line arguments given to the program. This is useful for command-line parsing or configuration purposes.

- **var()** and **set_var()**: These functions get and set the value of an environment variable.

- **current_dir()** and **set_current_dir()**: These manage the current working directory of the process.

Sample Program

Following is how you can use **std::env** to process command-line arguments, demonstrating not only retrieval but also basic usage in decision-making:

```
use std::env;


fn main() {

  let args: Vec<String> = env::args().collect();


  if args.len() > 1 {

  println!("Arguments passed: {:?}", &args[1..]);

  } else {

  println!("No arguments were passed.");

  }
```

```
}
```

How It Works?

- **env::args()**: Retrieves the arguments given to the program. The first argument is always the path to the program itself, so any additional arguments start from index 1.

- **collect()**: Converts the iterator into a vector so that it's easier to work with.

Sample Program

Another common use of the **std::env** module is to access environment variables, which can dictate runtime behavior without hard-coding values into the application.

```
use std::env;


fn main() {

 match env::var("MY_VARIABLE") {

 Ok(value) => println!("MY_VARIABLE: {}", value),

 Err(e) => println!("Couldn't read MY_VARIABLE ({})", e),

 }

}
```

The **std::env** module is critical for developing applications that need to interact robustly with their operating environment. It facilitates customization and flexibility, allowing the same application binary to behave differently based on external configurations such as command-line arguments or environment variables.

std::fmt

The **std::fmt** module provides functionality for formatting and printing text. It's particularly useful for customizing the way types are displayed and interacted with in textual form. We will learn through implementing custom formatting for a type using **std::fmt** and learn the key components that make this possible.

Customizing Textual Output

To define how a type should be formatted, you can implement traits from the **std::fmt** module. The most commonly used traits are:

- **fmt::Display**: For user-facing output, where you define a "to string" representation.

- **fmt::Debug**: For developer-facing output, typically auto-derived using **#[derive(Debug)]**, which gives a straightforward representation suitable for debugging.

Sample Program

To implement custom formatting, you define how your type should appear when used with formatting macros like **println!**. Given below is a step-by-step example to demonstrate custom formatting for a simple struct:

```rust
use std::fmt;


struct Point {
  x: i32,

  y: i32,

}


impl fmt::Display for Point {
  fn fmt(&self, f: &mut fmt::Formatter<'_>) -> fmt::Result {

  // Use the write! macro to write formatted output to the formatter

  write!(f, "Point({}, {})", self.x, self.y)

  }
```

```
}

fn main() {

 let point = Point { x: 7, y: 10 };

 println!("{}", point); // Outputs: Point(7, 10)

}
```

Key Elements

- **fmt::Formatter**: This is passed to the **fmt** method and handles the actual process of formatting.

- **fmt::Result**: This method returns a result that indicates whether the formatting was successful or if an error occurred during formatting.

std::str

The **std::str** module provides various functionalities to effectively manage and manipulate string data. One of the key functions available in this module is **from_utf8**, which is used to convert a byte slice into a string slice, ensuring that the byte slice is valid UTF-8.

Key Functions

The **from_utf8** function is essential for creating string slices from byte arrays, particularly when you are dealing with input or data that originates as bytes.

Following is how it works and why it's useful:

- **from_utf8** checks if the byte slice conforms to UTF-8 encoding rules. This is crucial because Rust's strings are UTF-8 by default, and ensuring this compliance avoids runtime errors and potential vulnerabilities related to invalid string content.

- This function returns a **Result<&str, Utf8Error>**. If the byte slice is valid UTF-8, it returns **Ok(&str)**, allowing safe usage of the data as a string. If the slice is not valid UTF-8, it returns an error (**Err(Utf8Error)**), which can then be handled appropriately in the code. This approach prevents your program from crashing and allows for more graceful error handling.

Sample Program

To demonstrate the practical application of **std::str::from_utf8**, consider a scenario where you are reading raw bytes from a file or network that should represent text:

```rust
use std::str;



fn main() {

 // Simulate reading bytes which are expected to be valid
UTF-8 text

 let bytes = [104, 101, 108, 108, 111]; // represents the
word "hello"



 // Attempt to convert bytes to a UTF-8 string slice

 match str::from_utf8(&bytes) {

 Ok(s) => println!("Converted string: {}", s),

 Err(e) => println!("Failed to convert bytes to string:
{}", e),

 }

}
```

In the above sample program,

- The **bytes** array is manually defined for simplicity, typically representing data you might receive from an external source.
- **str::from_utf8** is used to try converting the byte array to a string. If the bytes are valid UTF-8, it prints the string. Otherwise, it reports an error.
- This method showcases handling potential errors gracefully rather than unwrapping the result, which might cause the program to panic if the bytes are not valid UTF-8.

std::iter

The **std::iter** module is a powerhouse for creating and manipulating iterators and the iterators are used to lazily compute a sequence of values and provide a range of methods for transforming and consuming these sequences in an efficient manner.

Core Concepts

- Iterators: The cornerstone of this module, iterators have a couple of fundamental methods: **next**, which advances the iterator and returns an **Option** containing the next value, and **size_hint**, which provides an upper and lower bound on the remaining length of the iterator.

- Adaptors: These methods modify iterators to produce new iterators with different sequences or properties. Examples include **map**, which applies a function to each item of an iterator, and **filter**, which removes items that don't satisfy a predicate.

- Consumers: These methods consume iterators to produce a result, such as **fold**, **for_each**, and **collect**. Consumers are often used to accumulate results or apply side effects.

Sample Program

Rust's **std::iter** offers methods to create both infinite and finite iterators. One particularly useful function is **repeat**, which infinitely repeats a given value. Paired with **take**, which limits the number of items from an iterator, you can effectively create bounded sequences from infinite sources.

Following is a demonstration of how you might use these together:

```
use std::iter;


fn main() {

  // Create an iterator that repeats the number 5

  let repeated_fives = iter::repeat(5);



  // Use 'take' to get only the first 10 elements

  let limited_fives: Vec<i32> =
repeated_fives.take(10).collect();
```

```
 // The resulting vector contains the number 5, repeated
10 times

 println!("{:?}", limited_fives);

}
```

The **std::iter** module allows for high flexibility in generating and manipulating data sequences. It supports everything from simple loops to complex data pipelines that efficiently handle potentially large datasets. Iterators are central to Rust's zero-cost abstractions philosophy. They allow for loop fusion and other optimizations that often lead to faster programs compared to traditional loop constructs.

std::ops

The **std::ops** module implements operator overloading, allowing custom types to interact using traditional operator symbols like **+**, **−**, *****, etc. This capability enhances readability and maintains the intuitive nature of arithmetic or logical operations when applied to user-defined data types.

Overview

- The module provides a set of traits to define how specific operators behave for your types. For example, **Add** for **+**, **Sub** for **−**, **Mul** for *****, and so on. Each trait requires you to implement a method that defines the operation. For **Add**, this method is **add**, which returns the result of adding two instances of a type.

- These traits use associated types to specify the output type of the operation. In the case of **Add**, the associated type is **Output**, which determines the type returned by the **add** method.

Sample Program

To put this into practice, we consider a custom struct named **Vector** that represents a mathematical vector. You might want to enable adding two **Vector** instances using the **+** operator. Following is how you could implement this:

```
use std::ops::Add;
```

```rust
#[derive(Debug, PartialEq)]
struct Vector {
 x: i32,
 y: i32,
}


impl Add for Vector {
 type Output = Vector;


 fn add(self, other: Vector) -> Vector {
 Vector {
 x: self.x + other.x,
 y: self.y + other.y,
 }
 }
}


fn main() {
 let vector1 = Vector { x: 1, y: 2 };
 let vector2 = Vector { x: 3, y: 4 };
 let result = vector1 + vector2;
```

```
println!("{:?}", result); // Output will be Vector { x:
4, y: 6 }

}
```

Key Learning

- By overloading operators, you can make operations on custom types as intuitive and natural as those on primitive types.

- You have complete control over the semantics of the operations, enabling behaviors specific to the logic of your domain or application.

- Operator overloading with **std::ops** is type-safe, ensuring that only compatible operations are allowed at compile time, which reduces runtime errors.

std::fs

The **std::fs** module provides a robust and straightforward way to interact with the file system, ensuring that operations are both efficient and safe.

Basic File Reading

The **std::fs::File** type is used to open files for reading or writing. To read a file's content into a string efficiently, you can combine **File** with **std::io::BufReader**. **BufReader** buffers the input, reducing the number of read operations performed and potentially increasing performance when dealing with larger files.

Given below is a simple example that demonstrates reading from a file:

```
use std::fs::File;

use std::io::{self, BufReader, Read};


fn read_file_to_string(file_path: &str) ->
io::Result<String> {

  let file = File::open(file_path)?;

  let mut buf_reader = BufReader::new(file);
```

```rust
    let mut contents = String::new();

    buf_reader.read_to_string(&mut contents)?;

    Ok(contents)

}


fn main() -> io::Result<()> {

    match read_file_to_string("example.txt") {

    Ok(contents) => println!("File contents: {}", contents),

    Err(e) => println!("Error reading file: {}", e),

    }

    Ok(())

}
```

Writing to a File

Writing to a file is similarly straightforward. You can use **std::fs::File** along with **std::io::Write** to write data efficiently:

```rust
use std::fs::File;

use std::io::prelude::*;


fn write_to_file(file_path: &str, data: &str) ->
std::io::Result<()> {

    let mut file = File::create(file_path)?;

    file.write_all(data.as_bytes())?;
```

```
 Ok(())

}


fn main() -> std::io::Result<()> {

 write_to_file("output.txt", "Hello, world!")?;

 println!("Data written to file");

 Ok(())

}
```

Handling Errors with ?

Error handling is managed using the **Result** type, which can either be **Ok** indicating success or **Err** indicating an error. The **?** operator is used for error propagation, which simplifies the handling of errors in functions that return **Result**.

Modifying File Metadata

The **std::fs** module also allows you to modify file metadata, such as permissions:

```
use std::fs::{self, Permissions};

use std::os::unix::fs::PermissionsExt;


fn change_file_permissions(file_path: &str, perm: u32) ->
std::io::Result<()> {

 let metadata = fs::metadata(file_path)?;

 let mut permissions = metadata.permissions();

 permissions.set_mode(perm); // Unix-specific function
```

```
fs::set_permissions(file_path, permissions)?;

Ok(())

}


fn main() -> std::io::Result<()> {

change_file_permissions("example.txt", 0o644)?; // Read
and write for owner, read for others

println!("Permissions changed");

Ok(())

}
```

These above snippets highlight how **std::fs** and associated types facilitate detailed file and I/O operations to achieve performance and safety in programs and system applications.

Primitive Types

Primitive types are the foundational data types from which more complex structures are built. These types include integers, floating points, Booleans, and characters, each serving fundamental roles in data manipulation and program logic.

Understanding Rust's Primitive Types

Boolean (bool)

This is a simple type representing a value of either **true** or **false**. It's crucial for flow control and conditional statements.

Characters (char)

Rust's **char** type is four bytes in size and represents a Unicode Scalar Value, which can describe a lot more characters than ASCII can, including emoji.

Integer Types

Rust provides both signed (**i8**, **i16**, **i32**, **i64**, **i128**) and unsigned (**u8**, **u16**, **u32**, **u64**, **u128**) integers. The number in the type name indicates the number of bits each uses. For example, **i32** is a 32-bit signed integer.

Floating-Point Types (f32, f64)

Rust offers two floating-point types; **f32** and **f64**, which are single and double precision according to the IEEE-754 standard. They are primarily used for numerical computations that require decimal precision.

Size Types (isize, usize)

These types depend on the kind of system your program is running on. **usize** is typically used for indexing collections, and **isize** for counting items in a collection.

Sample Program

To illustrate, consider a simple function that uses these types:

```
fn main() {

  let flag: bool = true;

  let character: char = 'A';

  let integer: i32 = -123;

  let big_unsigned: u128 = 12345678901234567890;

  let float: f32 = 3.14;

  let double: f64 = 3.141592653589793;


  println!("Boolean value: {}", flag);

  println!("Character: {}", character);

  println!("Integer: {}", integer);

  println!("Big Unsigned: {}", big_unsigned);
```

```
println!("Float: {}", float);

println!("Double: {}", double);

}
```

In the above sample program, each type is declared with a specific value, demonstrating how simple data is managed in Rust. This function is especially helpful for understanding the direct application of primitive types. Primitive types are used in almost every aspect of programming from controlling logic with Booleans, managing text with characters, to performing calculations with integers and floating points.

Collections

Collections are versatile data structures that organize and store data efficiently, supporting a variety of operations. They are part of the Rust Standard Library and cater to different needs, from fixed-size arrays to dynamic hash maps. We shall explore deep into these collections, their characteristics, and their uses.

Arrays and Vectors

Arrays are fixed-size collections that store multiple items of the same type. They are allocated on the stack, which can be beneficial for performance when you know the size of your collection upfront and it's relatively small. For example:

```
let array = [1, 2, 3, 4, 5];
```

Vectors, on the other hand, are dynamic, growable arrays allocated on the heap. This flexibility allows you to append elements as needed:

```
let mut vector = Vec::new();

vector.push(1);

vector.push(2);

vector.push(3);
```

Slices

Slices are non-owning views into a sequence of elements, either part of an array or a vector. They are useful when you want to work with a subset of collection data without copying it:

```
let slice = &array[1..4]; // Slices from index 1 to index
3
```

Strings and String Slices

Strings are growable and stored on the heap, making them ideal for scenarios where you need to modify or extend text:

```
let mut s = String::from("hello");

s.push_str(", world!");
```

The **str** type, often referred to as string slices, is an immutable sequence of characters:

```
let greeting: &str = "hello";
```

HashMaps and HashSets

HashMaps are key-value stores that offer fast retrieval, insertion, and deletion of elements using hashing to manage keys:

```
let mut scores = HashMap::new();

scores.insert("Alice", 88);

scores.insert("Bob", 95);

let alice_score = scores.get("Alice");
```

HashSets, similar to hash maps but only store unique elements, making them perfect for operations like checking membership or ensuring no duplicates:

```
let mut books = HashSet::new();

books.insert("1984");
```

```
books.insert("Brave New World");

let has_nineteen_eighty_four = books.contains("1984");
```

These sets are essential for regular programming work and provide the groundwork for more advanced data structures. You can significantly impact the functionality and performance of your Rust applications by knowing when to use them based on their characteristics, such as fixed size vs. growable or ordered vs. unordered.

Macros

Macros are defined using **macro_rules!**, and they work by matching patterns of code against specified rules. Unlike functions, macros are expanded into source code that gets compiled along with the rest of the program, allowing them to perform tasks that are beyond the capabilities of functions.

Given below is a simple example of a macro that prints a message to the console:

```
macro_rules! say_hello {

  () => {

  println!("Hello!");

  };

}
```

This macro can be called using **say_hello!();** within a Rust program, and it expands into a call to **println!("Hello!");**.

Advantages of Using Macros

- Macros can generate complex code structures based on simpler input. This is particularly useful for reducing boilerplate code.

- Since macros are expanded at compile time, they allow you to include code that can perform checks and computations during compilation.

- They can accept a variable number of arguments, making them flexible in different situations.

Sample Program

Consider a macro used for logging. This macro can take variable input parameters and format them appropriately, which is more complex and flexible than what functions typically offer:

```
macro_rules! log {

 ($($arg:tt)*) => {

 println!("Log: {}", format_args!($($arg)*));

 };

}
```

This macro uses **format_args!**, a built-in macro used to handle formatting. The syntax **$(...)*** is used to denote that the macro accepts a variable number of arguments.

Parameterized Macros

Macros can be parameterized to generate more specific code based on the input. For example, a macro could generate function definitions:

```
macro_rules! create_function {

 ($func_name:ident) => {

 fn $func_name() {

 println!("Function {} is called",
stringify!($func_name));

 }

 };

}


create_function!(foo);
```

```
create_function!(bar);


fn main() {

  foo();

  bar();

}
```

In the above code snippet, **create_function!** macro generates two functions, **foo** and **bar**, each of which prints its own name when called. The **stringify!** macro is used to convert the identifier to a string.

Writing Your First Macro

As said earlier, macros are defined using the **macro_rules!** attribute. This allows you to write a kind of pattern-matching code that generates other Rust code during compilation.

Define Macro Name and Rule

Start with the **macro_rules!** followed by the name of the macro you want to create. The rules for the macro are enclosed in braces **{}**.

```
macro_rules! helpcode {

  () => {

  // Macro expansion contents go here

  };

}
```

Specify Macro Body

Inside the macro definition, you use **() => { ... }** to specify what the macro will expand into when it's called. This is where you put the code that the macro will output when used.

```
macro_rules! helpcode {

  () => {

  println!("For help with your code, try these
resources:");

  println!("- The Rust documentation: https://doc.rust-
lang.org/stable/");

  println!("- The Rust programming language book:
https://doc.rust-lang.org/stable/book/");

  // Additional resources can be added here

  };

}
```

Use Macro

To use the macro, simply call it like a function in your Rust code. Following is how you might call the **helpcode!** macro in your **main** function:

```
fn main() {

  helpcode!();

}
```

Once you've written your first macro, you'll be able to reuse those code snippets for future projects, which will boost your productivity and make your Rust code more maintainable.

Summary

In this chapter, we explored the Rust Standard Library in detail. The library provides a wide range of features that make Rust programming more powerful and efficient. From HashMaps-style collection handling to the std::error module for error management and std::net for network operations, we've covered it all. Notably, std::collections provided methods for efficiently handling complex data structures like vectors and hash maps, which are essential for managing dynamic data sets.

Making our programs more reliable by avoiding runtime panics with thoughtful error propagation and handling strategies, we gained insights into robust error handling through std::error, which leverages Rust's Result type.

In addition, the std::sync module demonstrated the safe use of state management in concurrent programming environments, specifically how to prevent data races using tools such as Arc and Mutex. In multi-threaded applications, this is of the utmost importance to ensure data safety and consistency.

We also learned how the std::time module can be used to work with durations and measure time, which improves the capacity to create applications that are performance-sensitive by enabling accurate time tracking and management.

Last but not least, learning about macros showed how useful they are for meta-programming, which involves automating code generation during compile time, decreasing boilerplate, and increasing code flexibility. Among Rust's notable features, this one makes it easier and more error-proof to implement complicated programming patterns.

CHAPTER 10: SMART POINTERS & REFERENCE CYCLES

Introduction

In Chapter 10, you will explore the scope of smart pointers in Rust, a fundamental feature that aids in the safe and flexible management of memory without the need for garbage collection. Various types of Rust smart pointers, including Box, Arc (Atomic Reference Counted), and Weak, will be covered in this chapter. All of these are essential for memory management, but they become even more important when working with complicated data structures that other parts of the program need to share or modify.

The chapter will include the basic concepts of smart pointers and how they enhance Rust's capability to handle memory efficiently. You'll learn about **Box** for allocating values on the heap, **Rc** for enabling multiple ownership of data, and **Arc** for sharing data safely across concurrent threads. **Weak** pointers will also be explored, which help prevent strong reference cycles that can lead to memory leaks.

Moreover, the chapter will cover the concept of reference cycles, explaining how they occur when two or more smart pointers reference each other in a cycle, making it impossible for Rust to automatically clean up the memory. You'll see practical examples on how to create and identify reference cycles, both between objects and more complex structures like classes.

Finally, you'll explore strategies to prevent these cycles, ensuring your Rust applications are efficient, safe, and free of memory leaks.

Understanding Smart Pointers

Smart pointers are more than just memory addresses; they encompass additional functionalities and safety guarantees that make them pivotal in memory management. Following are quick info of how they work and why they are beneficial:

- Box<T>: This is the simplest type of smart pointer. It allocates data on the heap and transfers ownership, which is particularly useful for large data structures or when you want to ensure data remains intact without copies as it moves throughout a program. The **Box** pointer automatically deallocates the heap memory when it goes out of scope, thanks to Rust's **Drop** trait, preventing memory leaks.

- Rc<T>: The Reference Counted smart pointer allows multiple ownership of data through reference counting. It enables multiple parts of your program to read data without taking full ownership of it, making **Rc<T>** ideal for use cases where data needs to be accessed by several parts simultaneously. However, because reference counts need to be adjusted at runtime, **Rc<T>** incurs a runtime cost. It's important to note that **Rc<T>** is not thread-safe and cannot be used in concurrent scenarios.

- Arc<T>: The Atomic Reference Counted pointer is similar to **Rc<T>** but is designed for a multi-threaded context. It uses atomic operations to adjust reference counts, ensuring that it remains thread-safe. **Arc<T>** is a bit slower than **Rc<T>** due to the overhead of thread safety mechanisms, but it is critical for sharing data across threads safely.

- Weak<T>: Sometimes, **Rc<T>** and **Arc<T>** can create cycles of references that lead to memory leaks because the reference count never reaches zero. **Weak<T>** pointers help avoid these cycles. They are a variant of **Rc<T>** and **Arc<T>** that hold a non-owning reference to the managed data. Unlike a strong reference, a **Weak** reference does not contribute to the reference count. This is crucial for cases where you might have cyclical references between values.

In order to manage memory effectively in Rust, it is essential to understand these smart pointers and how they each contribute to safe and efficient memory usage. By design, they protect Rust programs from typical mistakes like double frees and null pointer dereferencing, which is in line with Rust's promises of safety and concurrency that don't require a garbage collector.

Box<T>

The **Box<T>** smart pointer is a fundamental tool for managing heap-allocated data, allowing programmers to manage the scope and lifetime of objects in memory effectively. Given below is a more detailed look at how you can utilize **Box<T>**:

Basic Usage

A **Box** is typically used to store data on the heap rather than the stack. This is particularly useful for large data structures or when data needs to be transferred without performance overhead associated with copies. The creation of a **Box** is straightforward:

```
let b = Box::new(5);

println!("b = {}", b);
```

This allocates an integer on the heap, and **b** becomes the owner of this heap-allocated integer.

Ownership and Moves

A **Box** can take ownership of data and can be used to transfer ownership between functions or threads, ensuring data remains valid as long as needed. Consider this example where ownership is transferred:

```
let a = 5;

let b = Box::new(a);

let c = *b; // dereference to access the data

println!("c = {}", c); // 'b' is moved here
```

In this scenario, **b** takes ownership of the data from **a** and transfers it to **c**. After the transfer, **b** is no longer accessible.

Complex Data Structures

Box is also widely used for complex data structures, especially when dealing with recursive types or when a known size is necessary for types at compile time. Given below is an example with a custom data structure:

```
#[derive(Debug)]

struct Point {

 x: f64,

 y: f64,

}


let p = Box::new(Point { x: 1.0, y: 2.0 });

println!("p = {:?}", p);
```

This stores an instance of **Point** on the heap, making it easier to manage in memory-heavy operations or complex data manipulations.

Use with Traits and Polymorphism

Box is crucial when dealing with dynamic dispatch and polymorphism. It can hold trait objects allowing for runtime polymorphism. For example, if you have a trait **Drawable** and various structs implementing this trait, you can use **Box** to store instances of these structs and call methods dynamically.

Box<T> offers controlled and safe management of heap-allocated data with automatic cleanup, preventing memory leaks and ensuring that resources are freed when no longer needed. It exemplifies Rust's guarantees of memory safety without needing a garbage collector, allowing precise control over memory allocation and deallocation.

Rc<T>

The **Rc<T>** is a type of smart pointer known as a "reference counted" pointer which is used for managing memory in heap-allocated objects through reference counting. It enables multiple ownership of the same data, with the data being cleaned up when the last owner goes out of scope. Given below is a deeper look into its functionalities and usage:

Basic Usage

Rc<T> allows multiple parts of your program to read data stored in the heap, with the **Rc<T>** keeping track of how many references to the data exist. Given below is how you can create and use an **Rc<T>**:

```
use std::rc::Rc;


fn main() {

  let value = Rc::new(5);

  let other_reference = Rc::clone(&value);

  println!("value = {}, other_reference = {}", value,
other_reference);

}
```

Cloning References

When you call **Rc::clone(&value)**, you are not making a deep copy of the data, but merely incrementing the reference count. This is a shallow copy operation that allows you to have multiple pointers to the same data:

```rust
let original = Rc::new(5);

let cloned = Rc::clone(&original);
```

This is particularly useful when you need to access the same data in different parts of your program without taking ownership.

Using Rc<T> with Structs

Rc<T> can be used to share more complex data structures such as structs:

```rust
#[derive(Debug)]

struct Point {

  x: f64,

  y: f64,

}


fn main() {

  let point = Rc::new(Point { x: 1.0, y: 2.0 });

  let another_point = Rc::clone(&point);

  println!("point = {:?}, another_point = {:?}", point,
another_point);

}
```

While **Rc<T>** is great for certain use cases, it comes with limitations. For example, it's not thread-safe. If you need a reference counted type that can be used across threads, **Arc<T>** is the atomic variant of **Rc<T>** and can be used instead.

Additionally, since **Rc<T>** does not deallocate its inner object until all references are dropped, it can lead to memory leaks if not managed carefully, especially in the presence of reference cycles. These cycles happen when two or more **Rc<T>** pointers reference each other in a cycle. To mitigate this, Rust provides **Weak\<T>**, which is a non-owning but still linked reference, and you will learn it in upcoming sections of this chapter.

Arc\<T>

Arc\<T> stands for "Atomic Reference Counting" and is a type of smart pointer that manages memory through reference counting, where the count is kept safe for use across multiple threads using atomic operations. Given below is a deeper dive into how you can use **Arc\<T>** in concurrent Rust programs.

Basic Usage

To share data between threads securely without leading to race conditions, **Arc\<T>** is crucial. It ensures that data is not prematurely deallocated while it's still being accessed by another thread. Given below is a simple example:

```rust
use std::sync::Arc;

use std::thread;


fn main() {

  let number = Arc::new(5); // Wrap the number in an Arc

  let shared_number = number.clone(); // Clone the Arc


  let new_thread = thread::spawn(move || {

  println!("Number in thread: {}", shared_number);

  });


  new_thread.join().unwrap();

  println!("Number in main thread: {}", number);
```

```
}
```

The above code snippet demonstrates the basic functionality of **Arc<T>**, showing how it can be cloned and safely shared between the main thread and a new thread.

Complex Data Structures

Arc<T> can also be used to share more complex data structures across threads. Consider this example with a custom data structure:

```
use std::sync::Arc;

use std::thread;


#[derive(Debug)]

struct Point {

 x: f64,

 y: f64,

}


fn main() {

 let point = Arc::new(Point { x: 1.0, y: 2.0 });

 let point_clone = point.clone();


 let new_thread = thread::spawn(move || {

 println!("Point in thread: {:?}", point_clone);

 });
```

```
new_thread.join().unwrap();

println!("Point in main thread: {:?}", point);

}
```

In this case, **Arc<T>** is used to share an instance of **Point** between multiple threads. Each thread gets a clone of the **Arc**, and thus, the original **Point** is kept until all references are dropped.

Considerations

While **Arc<T>** is powerful, it does not prevent all concurrency problems. For example, it doesn't provide mutual exclusion, meaning you cannot modify data in **Arc<T>** safely without additional synchronization primitives like **Mutex**. Following is how you can combine **Arc<T>** with **Mutex<T>** to safely mutate shared data:

```
use std::sync::{Arc, Mutex};

use std::thread;


fn main() {

 let counter = Arc::new(Mutex::new(0)); // Wrap the
counter with Arc and Mutex


 let mut handles = vec![];


 for _ in 0..10 {

 let counter_clone = counter.clone();

 let handle = thread::spawn(move || {
```

```rust
let mut num = counter_clone.lock().unwrap(); // Lock the
mutex to access the data

*num += 1;

});

handles.push(handle);

}


for handle in handles {

handle.join().unwrap();

}


println!("Result: {}", *counter.lock().unwrap());

}
```

The above code snippet safely increments a shared counter using multiple threads, demonstrating how **Arc<T>** can be used effectively with **Mutex<T>** to manage mutable state in a concurrent environment.

Weak<T>

Understanding Weak<T>

Weak<T> is a type of pointer that holds a non-owning reference to the managed allocation. Unlike **Rc<T>**, which increments the reference count of the data it points to, **Weak<T>** does not affect the reference count. This means that an object can be deallocated even if some **Weak<T>** references still exist. The existence of **Weak<T>** references does not prevent the data from being dropped, and **Weak<T>** pointers can be upgraded to **Rc<T>** pointers if needed.

One primary use case for **Weak<T>** is in hierarchical structures where you need to safely refer to parent nodes without owning them. This prevents reference cycles where the parent owns the child and the child also owns the parent, which would lead to memory leaks because the reference count would never reach zero.

Sample Program

Given below is an example that illustrates using **Weak<T>** in a tree structure:

```rust
use std::rc::{Rc, Weak};

use std::cell::RefCell;


#[derive(Debug)]

struct Node {

 value: i32,

 parent: RefCell<Weak<Node>>,

 children: RefCell<Vec<Rc<Node>>>,

}


impl Node {

  fn new(value: i32) -> Rc<Node> {

  Rc::new(Node {

  value,

  parent: RefCell::new(Weak::new()),

  children: RefCell::new(vec![]),

  })
```

```rust
    }

    fn add_child(parent: &Rc<Node>, child_val: i32) {
        let child = Node::new(child_val);

child.parent.borrow_mut().replace(Rc::downgrade(parent));
        parent.children.borrow_mut().push(Rc::clone(&child));
    }
}


fn main() {
    let root = Node::new(1);
    Node::add_child(&root, 2);
    Node::add_child(&root, 3);


    println!("Root: {:?}", root);
    println!("First child: {:?}",
root.children.borrow()[0]);
    println!("Second child: {:?}",
root.children.borrow()[1]);
}
```

In the above sample program,

- Each **Node** contains a value, a **Weak** reference to its parent, and a list of children.

- The **parent** field uses **RefCell<Weak<Node>>** to allow mutable borrowing of an immutable **Node** structure, which is typical when combining **Rc** or **Weak**.

- Children are stored in an **Rc<Node>** inside a **RefCell** to allow mutation of the children vector.

- **Weak::new()** creates a new **Weak** pointer, and **Rc::downgrade** is used to create a **Weak** pointer from an **Rc**.

This setup avoids reference cycles by ensuring that child nodes do not own their parent, hence allowing the memory associated with the parent to be freed when there are no other **Rc** pointers to it. Meanwhile, children can still be accessed and modified safely.

Understanding Reference Cycles

What are Reference Cycles?

A reference cycle can happen when two or more objects reference each other through **Rc** or **Arc**, creating a loop that keeps each other's reference counts above zero indefinitely. Since Rust's garbage collection is based on reference counting (for **Rc** and **Arc**), these cycles prevent the involved objects from being deallocated naturally.

How Reference Cycles Occur?

Consider a parent-child relationship where both hold references to each other:

- A **parent** node might own some **child** nodes, and these children might back-reference their parent.

- If both references are strong (**Rc<T>** or **Arc<T>**), neither the parent nor the child can be dropped if they form a cycle, as their reference counts never reach zero.

Sample Program

Imagine a simple node structure where each node knows its parent and also owns its children:

```
use std::rc::{Rc, RefCell};



struct Node {
```

```rust
    value: i32,

    parent: RefCell<Weak<Node>>,

    children: RefCell<Vec<Rc<Node>>>,

}


impl Node {

  fn new(value: i32) -> Rc<Node> {

  Rc::new(Node {

  value,

  parent: RefCell::new(Weak::new()),

  children: RefCell::new(vec![]),

  })

  }


  fn add_child(parent: &Rc<Node>, child_val: i32) {

  let child = Node::new(child_val);

  *child.parent.borrow_mut() = Rc::downgrade(parent);

  parent.children.borrow_mut().push(Rc::clone(&child));

  }

}
```

In this structure:

- Each **Node** owns its children via **Rc**.

- It references its parent as a **Weak** pointer to avoid strong reference cycles.

Breaking Reference Cycles

To prevent reference cycles:

- Use **Weak<T>** pointers for "back-references" or non-owning relationships, like the parent in a node. **Weak<T>** does not increment the reference count.

- Regularly analyze and refactor code to ensure that ownership structures are acyclic where possible.

Detecting and Handling Cycles

Identifying reference cycles might be difficult in the absence of appropriate tools. There are no in-built tools in Rust that can detect these cycles during runtime or compilation. To prevent these problems, developers should carefully plan their architecture and how they will use pointers. It may be helpful to use external libraries or tools that are specifically made for memory profiling and leak detection in complex applications where cycles are more common. These can help you find the problematic areas in your code.

Types of Reference Cycles

Reference Cycles Between Objects

This type of reference cycle occurs within structures where objects are mutually referencing each other. Common examples include graph data structures, trees, and doubly-linked lists, where nodes might have links to their parents as well as their children. These cycles make it difficult for Rust's automatic memory management to clean up properly because the reference count never reaches zero, thus preventing the **Drop** trait from being called and the memory from being freed.

To handle these situations, Rust provides the **Weak<T>** pointer type, which allows one to hold a reference to an object without owning it outright. This prevents the increment of the reference count. Given below is a simple program using a tree structure:

```
use std::rc::{Rc, Weak};

use std::cell::RefCell;
```

```rust
struct Node {
  value: i32,
  parent: RefCell<Weak<Node>>,
  children: RefCell<Vec<Rc<Node>>>,
}

impl Node {
  fn new(value: i32) -> Rc<Node> {
  Rc::new(Node {
  value,
  parent: RefCell::new(Weak::new()),
  children: RefCell::new(vec![]),
  })
  }

  fn add_child(parent: &Rc<Node>, value: i32) {
  let new_child = Node::new(value);
  *new_child.parent.borrow_mut() = Rc::downgrade(parent);

parent.children.borrow_mut().push(Rc::clone(&new_child));
  }
```

```
}
```

In this setup, **parent** is a **Weak\<Node>**, preventing a strong reference cycle when a parent has references to its children and vice versa.

Reference Cycles Between Objects and Closures

These cycles often occur when closures capture **Rc** or **Arc** pointers to objects that also own the closures. This pattern is frequent in GUI development or asynchronous programming where callbacks are involved. The closure captures the environment by reference, and if those references include the object owning the closure, a cycle is created.

To illustrate, consider a simplified scenario involving a GUI element that updates its state using a closure:

```
use std::rc::Rc;

use std::cell::RefCell;


struct GuiElement {

  state: RefCell<i32>,

  on_click: RefCell<Option<Rc<dyn Fn()>>>,

}


impl GuiElement {

  fn new() -> Rc<GuiElement> {

  Rc::new(GuiElement {

  state: RefCell::new(0),

  on_click: RefCell::new(None),

  })
```

```
}

fn set_on_click<F: 'static + Fn()>(self: &Rc<Self>, f:
F) {

*self.on_click.borrow_mut() = Some(Rc::new(f));

}


fn click(&self) {

if let Some(ref callback) = *self.on_click.borrow() {

callback();

}

}

}


fn main() {

let button = GuiElement::new();

let button_clone = Rc::clone(&button);

button.set_on_click(move || {

*button_clone.state.borrow_mut() += 1;

println!("Button clicked, state now: {}",
button_clone.state.borrow());

});
```

```
button.click();

button.click();

}
```

In the above, **button_clone** is an **Rc** that captures the button itself, leading to a potential cycle if not carefully managed. Using **Weak<T>** instead of **Rc<T>** for such scenarios can prevent these cycles, as the weak pointer does not contribute to the reference count.

These two cases illustrate how Rust deals with memory safety and the importance of developers being careful with references and ownership in order to prevent leaks and unexpected behavior in bigger applications.

Creating Reference Cycle Between Objects

Understanding reference cycles between objects is essential for ensuring that your applications manage memory efficiently and avoid memory leaks. To demonstrate how to create such cycles and explore their implications, we now look at an example involving a tree data structure.

Sample Program

Reference cycles often occur when using smart pointers like **Rc<T>**. A simple example might involve a tree where each node has a reference to its children, and potentially back to its parent, forming a cyclic reference:

```
use std::rc::Rc;

use std::cell::RefCell;


struct TreeNode {

  value: i32,

  parent: RefCell<Weak<TreeNode>>,
```

```rust
    children: RefCell<Vec<Rc<TreeNode>>>,
}


impl TreeNode {
    fn new(value: i32) -> Rc<TreeNode> {
    Rc::new(TreeNode {
    value,
    parent: RefCell::new(Weak::new()),
    children: RefCell::new(vec![]),
    })
    }


    fn add_child(parent: &Rc<TreeNode>, child_value: i32) ->
Rc<TreeNode> {
    let child = TreeNode::new(child_value);
    *child.parent.borrow_mut() = Rc::downgrade(parent);
    parent.children.borrow_mut().push(Rc::clone(&child));
    child
    }
}
```

In this code:

- Each **TreeNode** has a value and potential children.

- It uses **Rc** for shared ownership of children and **Weak** to prevent strong reference cycles via the parent link, which helps avoid memory leaks.

The **Weak** type is crucial in preventing strong reference cycles. While **Rc** increments the reference count, ensuring that an object is not deallocated prematurely, **Weak** does not. This allows a node's parent to be dropped independently of its children, breaking potential cycles.

Creating Cyclic Linked List

Creating a cyclic linked list can also be illustrative:

```
fn main() {

 let first = Rc::new(RefCell::new(TreeNode::new(1)));

 let second = Rc::new(RefCell::new(TreeNode::new(2)));

 let third = Rc::new(RefCell::new(TreeNode::new(3)));


 first.borrow_mut().next = Some(Rc::clone(&second));

 second.borrow_mut().next = Some(Rc::clone(&third));

 third.borrow_mut().next = Some(Rc::clone(&first)); //
Creates a cycle here

}
```

This linked list has each node pointing to the next, with the last node pointing back to the first, creating a cycle. While **Rc** helps manage shared ownership, cycles like these mean the reference count never reaches zero, preventing proper deallocation. In the above, without intervention, Rust's memory safety guarantees do not prevent memory leakage; thus, careful management of **Rc** and **Weak** pointers is crucial.

Creating Reference Cycle Between Objects & Closure

Complex structures, such as event loops or asynchronous tasks, make the creation of a reference cycle between objects and closures more nuanced. A circular reference is the result, in general, of an object holding a reference to a closure, which is then captured by the object itself.

Sample Program

For example, consider a scenario where you have a task that needs to execute some operation after a certain condition is met, and this operation involves accessing the object that scheduled the task. Given below is how you might structure such a scenario using **Rc** and a closure:

```rust
use std::rc::{Rc, Weak};

use std::cell::RefCell;


struct Task {

 value: i32,

 // Using a closure that potentially captures an Rc
reference

 on_complete: RefCell<Option<Box<dyn Fn()>>>,

}


impl Task {

 fn new(value: i32) -> Rc<Self> {

 Rc::new(Task {

 value,

 on_complete: RefCell::new(None),

 })

 }
```

```rust
fn set_on_complete<F>(&self, callback: F)

where

F: Fn() + 'static,

{

*self.on_complete.borrow_mut() =
Some(Box::new(callback));

}


fn run_callbacks(&self) {

if let Some(callback) =
self.on_complete.borrow_mut().take() {

callback();

}

}

}


fn main() {

let task = Task::new(10);

let task_clone = Rc::clone(&task);


// Setting a closure that captures `task_clone`
```

```
task.set_on_complete(move || {

println!("Task completed with value: {}",
task_clone.value);

});



// This would potentially cause a cycle since
`task_clone` captures `task`

task.run_callbacks();

}
```

In the above sample program,

- The **Task** struct includes a callback that gets executed under certain conditions.

- We define a closure that captures an **Rc** clone of the task, which could potentially lead to a reference cycle if not managed correctly.

To mitigate such reference cycles, especially in cases where you have an object capturing itself through closures, you can use **Weak** pointers. A **Weak** pointer references an **Rc** without increasing its reference count:

```
use std::rc::{Rc, Weak};

use std::cell::RefCell;



fn main() {

let task = Task::new(10);

let weak_task = Rc::downgrade(&task);



// Setting a closure that captures a `Weak` reference
```

```
task.set_on_complete(move || {

if let Some(task) = weak_task.upgrade() {

println!("Task completed with value: {}", task.value);

}

});



// No cycle since `weak_task` does not increase the
reference count

task.run_callbacks();

}
```

In the above adjusted program:

- We use **Weak::downgrade** to create a **Weak** reference that the closure captures.

- Inside the closure, we attempt to upgrade the **Weak** reference to an **Rc**. If the original **Rc** still exists, it executes the code within the closure; otherwise, it does nothing.

Preventing Reference Cycles

The two main strategies to prevent these reference cycles are the use of **Weak<T>** pointers and the restructuring of your data types to break potential cycles.

Using Weak References

Weak<T> pointers are a way to hold a reference to a value without owning it outright, which is crucial in preventing cycles especially in reference-counted data structures like those using **Rc<T>**. When you use a **Weak<T>**, it doesn't contribute to the reference count, so even if two objects reference each other, they can still be collected if there are no strong (**Rc<T>**) references keeping them alive.

Given below is a practical example to illustrate how **Weak<T>** can be used to prevent a reference cycle:

```rust
use std::rc::{Rc, Weak};

use std::cell::RefCell;


struct Node {

 value: i32,

 parent: RefCell<Weak<Node>>,

 children: RefCell<Vec<Rc<Node>>>,

}


impl Node {

 fn new(value: i32) -> Rc<Node> {

 Rc::new(Node {

 value,

 parent: RefCell::new(Weak::new()),

 children: RefCell::new(vec![]),

 })

 }


 fn add_child(parent: &Rc<Node>, child: Rc<Node>) {

 *child.parent.borrow_mut() = Rc::downgrade(parent);

 parent.children.borrow_mut().push(child);
```

```
  }

}


fn main() {

  let root = Node::new(1);

  let child1 = Node::new(2);

  let child2 = Node::new(3);


  Node::add_child(&root, child1);

  Node::add_child(&root, child2);

}
```

In the above sample program, each node has a **Weak** reference to its parent, which prevents a strong reference cycle that could lead to memory leaks. The **children** are held in **Rc<Node>**, allowing shared ownership among multiple parts of the program.

Breaking the Circular References

Another strategy to prevent reference cycles is by redesigning your data structures so that circular references are broken. This might mean changing how ownership is modeled within the structure. For instance, in doubly-linked lists, instead of two **Rc<T>** pointers (one in each direction), you might use one **Rc<T>** for forward links and **Weak<T>** for backward links.

```
struct Node {

  value: i32,

  next: Option<Rc<Node>>,

  prev: Option<Weak<Node>>,
```

```rust
}

impl Node {
 fn append(node: &Rc<Node>, value: i32) -> Rc<Node> {
 let new_node = Rc::new(Node {
 value,
 prev: Some(Rc::downgrade(node)),
 next: None,
 });

 if let Some(ref next) = node.next {
 next.prev = Some(Rc::downgrade(&new_node));
 }

 node.next = Some(new_node.clone());
 new_node
 }
}
```

You can avoid reference cycles and better manage memory in your Rust programs by using these strategies. System programming and other applications that rely on memory performance greatly benefit from this improvement in memory safety and efficiency.

Summary

As we wrap up our look at Rust, this chapter delves into reference cycles and smart pointers, two key ideas for efficient memory management in the programming language. It introduces various smart pointers like **Box<T>**, **Rc<T>**, **Arc<T>**, and **Weak<T>**, each designed to manage data differently, ensuring efficient resource handling. **Box<T>** is employed for heap allocation, **Rc<T>** for enabling multiple ownerships within a single-threaded context, **Arc<T>** extends **Rc<T>**'s functionalities to multithreaded scenarios, and **Weak<T>** helps in preventing reference cycles that could lead to memory leaks.

The book teaches how reference cycles occur when smart pointers create loops of ownership, thus preventing Rust's automatic memory cleanup features from collecting unused data. It provides practical examples, such as constructing reference cycles between objects and between objects and closures, which are common in complex data structures and asynchronous programming. Solutions to these cycles involve using **Weak<T>** pointers to weaken the connections within cycles or reorganizing data structures to avoid cyclic dependencies altogether.

You will walk away from this book with an extensive understanding of Rust's method for memory safety, which involves manual memory management techniques and helpful hints. If you want to build efficient apps that can withstand typical programming errors like memory leaks, these insights are essential.

Index

Epilogue

As we wrap up "Rust In Practice, Second Edition," I want to take a moment to appreciate the process we've gone through thus far, delving into all the features and complexities of the Rust programming language. Inspiring both theoretical knowledge and hands-on experience with Rust and its rich environment were two of the primary goals in writing this book. We covered Rust's distinctive characteristics and its method for addressing typical programming problems in a way that prioritizes performance and safety throughout the chapters.

From the fundamentals of ownership and borrowing—the building blocks of Rust's memory safety guarantees—to the ins and outs of concurrency, async programming, and smart pointers, there is a lot to cover. Through these chapters, I hope you have gained a better understanding of Rust's capabilities and have been inspired to incorporate them into your own projects.

The goal of the chapters on Cargo, Crates, and Rust's extensive standard library was to provide you with the necessary knowledge and skills to make full use of Rust's package management and its extensive set of pre-built features. At this point, you should have no trouble navigating Rust's modular approach to software development, which allows you to create programs that are both scalable and easy to maintain.

Our chapters of reference cycles and smart pointers was also an effort to provide you the tools you need to take on the more difficult parts of Rust programming. To avoid frequent mistakes like data races and memory leaks while developing high-performance applications, it is essential to have a solid grasp of these advanced concepts.

I hope that you will all keep exploring Rust, adding it to your projects, and being an active member of the Rust community as we wrap up this edition. Rust is a dynamic environment that is always changing thanks to its expanding ecosystem and welcoming community.

To all the developers out there, whether you're new to Rust or just want to brush up on your abilities, I hope this book is a reliable resource. Never stop pushing yourself, never stop learning, and always be ready to adapt; mastery is a journey that begins with a challenge.

It is my pleasure that you have decided to use this book as a guide as you learn to develop in Rust. Cheers to many more lines of efficiently written, concurrent code that is securely implemented.

Thank You

Made in United States
Troutdale, OR
09/28/2024